CLEOPATRA

Pat Southern

CLEOPATRA

Pat Southern

TEMPUS

First published 1999

PUBLISHED IN THE UNITED KINGDOM BY:

Tempus Publishing Ltd
The Mill, Brimscombe Port
Stroud, Gloucestershire GL5 2QG

PUBLISHED IN THE UNITED STATES OF AMERICA BY:

Tempus Publishing Inc.
2A Cumberland Street
Charleston, SC 29401

Tempus books are available in France, Germany and Belgium
from the following addresses:

Tempus Publishing Group	Tempus Publishing Group	Tempus Publishing Group
21 Avenue de la République	Gustav-Adolf-Straße 3	Place de L'Alma 4/5
37300 Joué-lès-Tours	99084 Erfurt	1200 Brussels
FRANCE	GERMANY	BELGIUM

British Library Cataloguing in Publication Data.
A catalogue record for this book is available from the British Library.

ISBN 0 7524 1435 6

Typesetting and origination by Tempus Publishing.
PRINTED AND BOUND IN GREAT BRITAIN.

Contents

For Graeme, with millions of thanks

Acknowledgements

This book probably began long ago when the films that they don't make any more regularly hit the screens of provincial cinemas. The author (then young) was an avid and somewhat repetitive film-goer with access to libraries and second-hand bookshops, acquiring an assortment of tomes with which to check out the details. The current volume owes its origin to the persistence of Peter Kemmis Betty, who suggested if I was going to write about Mark Antony I might as well write about Cleopatra. There are several people to thank, starting with Graeme Stobbs who draws maps from my incomprehensible bits of paper, and does so very quickly. Then there are the library staff at the University of Newcastle upon Tyne, the Inter-library loan staff at the Literary and Philosophical Society of Newcastle upon Tyne, and latterly the Trafford Metropolitan Borough Library Service. Jacqui Taylor produced drawings at short notice, listened patiently, and discussed details over tea and buns, as the book was emerging. David Brearley provided essential photos. The following Museums also kindly supplied photographs: Ny Carlsberg Glyptotek, Copenhagen; Vatican Museums, Vatican City; Cherchel Museum, Algeria; British Museum, London; Capitoline Museum, Rome.

List of illustrations

Introduction

Cleopatra is one of the most famous women, if not the most famous of all, of the ancient world, but her story is mostly legendary, full of fantastic anecdotes, based on reality but elaborated beyond the bounds of belief. Much of what we know of her descends from the propaganda spread abroad by Octavian, who made war on her and indirectly on Antony to gain supremacy for himself. When he became Augustus, Octavian could afford to relent a little. Having blackened her name as an enemy of Rome, after her death he recognised her nobility and courage. Perhaps this double-sided message, current in Augustus' own lifetime, is the source of the mixed feelings about Cleopatra today. For some she is still the evil temptress, full of restless ambition; for others she is a brave Queen who fell victim to an ambition greater than her own.

To write the story of Cleopatra it is also necessary to write about the lives of Caesar, Antony and Octavian, for many of their activities affected Egypt, and the wealth of Egypt had no little bearing on their careers. This would have been almost the same if Cleopatra had been a man, because Rome and Egypt were already inextricably linked. But she was a woman, and both Caesar and Antony went beyond diplomatic exchanges with her. It does not seem that she was promiscuous, and there are no recorded lovers besides these two illustrious Romans. She may have used them to gain her own ends with Roman support, but she was permanently loyal to them and their memories; had she been the self-centered, ambitious ruler of her legend she would have changed her allegiances when it suited her, whenever she was presented with opportunities to betray them for her own advantage.

As Queen of Egypt, Cleopatra was a conscientious ruler who cared for her people's well-being. She was the first of the Ptolemies to learn to speak the Egyptian language, and she fostered the ancient religion by attending ceremonies in person and continuing the Ptolemaic tradition of restoring temples, representing herself as Isis and her son Caesarion as Horus. She broke with tradition in establishing herself as sole ruler, whereas her Macedonian predecessors had always followed the tradition of the Pharaohs in brother-sister marriages, and in always having a Royal consort. Whether or not she married Caesar according to Egyptian rites, and then Antony, is unknown. Unofficially she perhaps thought of her Roman lovers as consorts, and remained faithful to them by not taking an Egyptian husband. In her youth, all that she had known of her brothers and sisters was faction and strife, ending in bloodshed. Besides, as sole ruler she could achieve much more without the hindrance of a second set of courtiers and advisers all advocating different ideas. In Rome Caesar had also reached the conclusion that sole rule was more efficient, and in the end this caused his downfall. No wonder the Romans looked askance on the autocratic tendencies of the Egyptian Queen, which proved so useful to Octavian when he began to convince his audience that she intended to take over the whole world. That was probably not her aim; she wanted a strong Egypt, and prosperity for her children and her people. Her Imperialistic methods were no more savage than Rome's, but she was portrayed as insatiable, greedy for more and more power. It was her misfortune that her wishes clashed with Rome's, or more precisely with the ambitions of one Roman who saw more clearly than most how to organise the world.

1 The Princess becomes a Queen

When Alexander the Great died in 323BC the huge Empire he had won and welded together lost its cohesion as his immediate associates went on to create kingdoms for themselves out of the territories he had conquered. These Successor kingdoms, some of them long-lasting dynasties surviving for centuries, others less fortunate, superimposed to a greater or lesser extent a Greek administration upon existing forms, taking over local institutions and customs intact, or adapting them to the wider purpose of government.

Alexander's friend Ptolemy Soter took charge of, or more accurately kidnapped, the body of his erstwhile general and conveyed it to Egypt, where he forcibly took over from Cleomenes, the appointed Macedonian administrator. Egypt was a wise choice. It was defensible and self-contained, fertile, and wealthy, all factors which ensured that three centuries later the growing power of Rome, or more specifically the growing power of one or two individual Romans, would eventually lead to its total absorption.

For the first two decades of his reign Ptolemy Soter made no territorial advances, concentrating instead on defending his kingdom against the aggression and acquisitive urges of his rivals. By the beginning of the third century BC he was able to extend his power over Cyprus and the Aegean islands, important for trade and control over weaker neighbouring powers. In Egypt itself he amalgamated Macedonian administration and Egyptian practices. He made Greek the official legal and administrative language without obliterating the native Egyptian language, culture, or religion. He observed all the ceremonial of Greek kings but ensured that he and his successors also observed the ancient ceremonials of the Pharaohs, providing an almost seamless join between the old and new rulers. He respected Egyptian tradition, inward-looking though it sometimes was, and he also brought Egypt into closer contact with the Mediterranean world when he moved the capital from Memphis to Alexandria, founded by and named after Ptolemy's hero Alexander, whose body lay there in regal state.

The Macedonian Ptolemaic dynasty survived through the reigns of another thirteen successors, all named Ptolemy, but with the useful addition of a secondary distinguishing name, such as the third Ptolemy known as Euergetes, which means 'Benefactor', or the twelfth Ptolemy nicknamed Auletes, or 'Flute-player', the father of Cleopatra. A granite sphinx with the head of Auletes was found in the harbour of Alexandria in 1998, during the ongoing underwater excavations there.

The reputation of this unfortunate individual is far from sound, up to a point perhaps even deservedly so. Though he has his apologists who recognise in his policies sensible aims and plans for the development of Egypt, to a large extent self-interest seems to have ruled him, to the eventual detriment of his country. Money slipped through his fingers faster than water, so he borrowed money from whoever would lend it, principally wealthy Romans, and then he borrowed again from other Romans to repay his original loans. If he had lived in modern times, credit cards, bank loans, and loans to pay off other loans, would have engendered a euphoric gleam in his eyes. Seemingly debts did not worry him since, after all, he had the wealth of Egypt behind him to pay them off. However, the drain of his country's resources in this fashion could not go unchallenged by the inhabitants of that country, who perhaps did not care for the wider issues that Ptolemy XII faced, and perceived only that the fruits of their labours were regularly siphoned off for no other purpose than the continued comfort and enjoyment of their ruler. Ptolemy XII Auletes may have suffered from a bad press in both ancient and modern times but he seems to have possessed one or two redeeming features, and when she became Queen of Egypt, Cleopatra was loyal to his memory. Had he been entirely incompetent or uncaring, it would not have been a shrewd policy for his daughter, newly established as ruler, to remind people of her ancestry. Perhaps circumstances and context were against Auletes, since Egypt was not under dire threat requiring his intervention; consequently he could not so easily display any pronounced military or diplomatic skills which would obliterate other deficiencies. A few resounding successes in either of these fields may have tempered his other faults.

When Ptolemy XII Auletes came to power in 80BC, Roman interests in him and his kingdom were well established; Rome was already deeply involved in the political and economic aspects of Egyptian affairs, and watchful for any opportunity to interfere. Auletes' predecessor had enjoyed only a very brief reign, installed by Lucius Cornelius Sulla and murdered by the Alexandrians in the same year. Succeeding him, Ptolemy Auletes made friendly overtures to Rome, and survived for over two decades with Roman support, but in 58 his debts and his close association with this dangerously acquisitive foreign power displeased the Alexandrians, who forced him to flee. Naturally he went to Rome, as the guest of those to whom he owed virtually everything, including money, his throne and even his life.

One of his main supporters was Gnaeus Pompeius Magnus, or Pompey the Great, the foremost general of his day and almost the only power that mattered in Rome, but Pompey did not want to become directly involved with Auletes and his problems on a personal level, so in 55BC when there was a rebellion in Egypt led by Auletes' daughter Berenice, Pompey employed his delegates to do the actual work of suppressing it and reinstating Ptolemy. He asked his loyal subordinate Aulus Gabinius, currently the governor of Syria, to take troops into Egypt, quell the court factions, and ensure that Ptolemy Auletes acquired and retained power. Gabinius marched into Judaea first, on more or less the same quest of placing rulers favourable to Rome on disputed thrones. This expedition was dubious in the extreme, especially when Gabinius did not simply conclude the business in Judaea and then return to base, but instead pounced on Egypt. As governor of Syria he had no rights to enter other territories without orders from the Senate, but he was acting on instructions from Pompey, who failed to defend him resolutely when he was prosecuted on his return to Rome. Some would say that Pompey sacrificed Gabinius to political correctness at a time when his own influence was waning, but at least he hired the best orator in Rome to take up the case for the defence. Pompey persuaded Cicero to take up the defence, but unfortunately for Gabinius it was all to no avail. The opposition was too strong.

The whole episode and apparent coup d'état of 56–55 in Egypt is mysterious because of a lack of reliable sources, which are in any case

1   *Coin of Ptolemy Auletes, Cleopatra's father.* © *British Museum*

biased towards the interests of Rome. Berenice was the second of Ptolemy's six known children (there may have been more), and though she seized power in 56, Rome merely watched events without doing very much. Apparently it was only when she married Archelaus of Pontus that it was felt that there might be some threat to Roman stability. This provided the excuse to interfere, conveniently removing Ptolemy from the city of Rome and out of Pompey's immediate circle, installing him as a friendly ruler in his rich country with every reason to be grateful and compliant not just to Rome in general but to Pompey the Great in particular.

When Gabinius arrived with his troops, there was some skirmishing, but it was soon over. Berenice was executed. The rest of the family may or may not have been implicated in the attempt to oust Auletes, but it is perhaps unlikely that all the siblings could act in concert for any length of time without squabbles. The eldest daughter, Cleopatra VI Tryphaena may have died or been removed before the rebellion even started. The two surviving boys, both named Ptolemy, were just young children, and the younger girls were adolescents, Arsinoe aged about eleven, and Cleopatra, the seventh of that name, about fourteen. This Cleopatra is the most famous of all the Ptolemaic Queens, and also has the distinction of being the last of her line before Octavian-Augustus seized Egypt for his own requirements, under the guise of making it a Roman province. Cleopatra VII was no late developer. From the start she seems to have been intelligent, widely educated, and politically aware. She may have accompanied her father to Rome and lived there from 58–55, — formative years for her from the age of about ten to fourteen. Her whereabouts and activities for these years are not recorded, and her loyalties are just as mysterious. The death of her sister Berenice could have affected her deeply, or it could have left her totally unmoved. Later, when she was established as Queen, she allegedly pronounced her sister disloyal, but that may have been an opinion derived from political necessity rather than personal emotion. Perhaps she learned very early the value of tacit neutrality until the proper time for revealing her hand, when she was certain of success. At fourteen she was old enough, and probably shrewd enough, to realise precisely what was going on, and above all to understand the overriding economic and political motives behind Pompey's interests in Egypt, and indeed all the other powerful Romans who followed in his wake. Above all, she cannot have failed to notice that the reinstatement of her father as ruler of Egypt with Roman backing, combined with the removal of her elder sister Berenice and the very young ages of her brothers, now made her an important and potentially powerful individual.

The extent to which Auletes may have been preparing Cleopatra for eventual succession to his throne is uncertain. Retrospective evidence, taken out of context, suggests that Cleopatra was always in line for the succession, and no doubt knew of it. The author of the *Alexandrian War*, probably Hirtius using notes left by Caesar, says that Auletes declared in his will that he wished the country to be ruled by his elder son Ptolemy and his daughter Cleopatra, and moreover Auletes appealed to the Roman people to honour and uphold this wish. This may be Caesarean propaganda, to advertise to both Egyptians and Romans that

2   *Head of Gnaeus Pompeius Magnus, better known as Pompey the Great. He*
    supported Ptolemy Auletes and was financially involved with Egyptian affairs. He
    was made guardian of the Royal children when Auletes died, and came to
    Alexandria after he was defeated at the battle of Pharsalus, expecting to raise money
    and supplies to continue the civil war with Caesar, but he was killed on the orders
    of Achillas, the commander of the army of Ptolemy XIII. Courtesy Ny Carlsberg
    Glyptotek

when he appointed Cleopatra as Queen of Egypt he had the backing of the legitimate testimony of the last ruler. The Egyptians would more likely acquiesce if they believed that the decision to promote Cleopatra derived from the declared intentions of Ptolemy XII rather than an uninvited Roman general, and the Roman people would also acquiesce in the decisions taken by Caesar if they imagined that they had a part to play in these measures. Conjecture about the intentions of Ptolemy Auletes and the motives of Julius Caesar will not alter the fact that, whether she was actively promoted or not, from 55 onwards Cleopatra was the eldest among four surviving children in line for the throne of Egypt, and will have accordingly made definite plans of her own concerning her survival and rank when her father died.

Conscious of her elevated but precarious position, and wary of upsetting the Alexandrians by too deep or obvious a relationship with the visiting Romans who had replaced her father on the throne, Cleopatra may not have deigned to notice Aulus Gabinius or his dashing young cavalry officer who was currently impressing all of Alexandria with his reckless generosity, Herculean drinking prowess and athletic form. Marcus Antonius, better known as Mark Antony, was twenty-five years old. He had spearheaded the invasion from Syria, capturing Pelusium on the east of the Delta before the rest of Gabinius's army had arrived, and more importantly he had kept the peace between Auletes and the supporters of Berenice, preventing a revengeful massacre or the outbreak of a fresh civil war. Antony hailed from a highly impoverished Roman aristocratic family, whose misfortune had been consistently to choose the wrong side in the various political struggles that beset Rome. He had an undistinguished past behind him and an uncertain future before him. He was already known as a reprobate; he had no personal fortune, but lots of debts, no important or influential supporters in Rome, but lots of disreputable friends. Seemingly devoid of any burning ambition to rule the world, Antony threw himself passionately into whatever fate decreed for him, and he lived life to the full. He appreciated a feminine form as much as and probably more than the next man, but being a realist his aspirations at this time probably did not reach as far as a lifelong involvement with a princess of the Nile. Similarly the ambitions of the aforementioned princess probably did not include bestowing her favours on a well-built, hard-drinking cavalry officer with no political influence or economic stability. Antony and Cleopatra had nothing to offer each other at this stage. If they met at all in those days, it would be on a formal and very restricted basis, and they would each have noted a name and a face, little more.

The presence of Roman troops in Egypt lent support to Auletes during the last years of his reign. The soldiers of Gabinius' army who remained behind after Gabinius himself returned to Syria contracted marriages with local women and raised families. To the Romans this was a shocking dereliction of duty, since soldiers were forbidden to marry, and marriage between Roman citizens and foreigners was illegal. From Auletes' point of view the liaisons between Roman soldiers and native women was an advantage because it lent cohesion and stability to the Roman units, which he incorporated into his own army and employed with success. In his account of the Alexandrian war after the defeat of Pompey, Caesar hints at some sort of civil strife, when he says that the soldiers of Gabinius fought the Egyptians on behalf of Auletes. It is unlikely that this refers to a serious civil war. There may have been discontent and rioting occasioned by Auletes' financial demands and those of the grasping Roman moneylenders, involving the Roman soldiers in police work and crowd-control.

At the beginning of the year 51 Auletes may have fallen ill. He died, probably in the early spring of that year, but the precise month is unknown. Evidence from papyrus records indicates that the thirtieth and final regnal year of Auletes was also counted jointly as the first year of Cleopatra's reign, implying that for a brief period there was in fact a joint reign. Normal Ptolemaic procedure was to begin new dating all over again when one ruler died and another succeeded, so the papyrus evidence does not simply mean that in the same year Auletes died and Cleopatra succeeded him. Something more significant is implied, perhaps that Auletes recognised that his time was short and wished to declare quite unequivocally that his heir was to be Cleopatra by making her co-ruler while he still lived. More sinister interpretations have been advanced, for instance Michael Grant suggests that Cleopatra may have kept the death of her father secret until she was established as Queen. Whatever the truth of the matter, for a short period Cleopatra seems to have ruled alongside her father, then for a short period alone, and finally she was joint ruler with her ten-year-old younger brother Ptolemy XIII.

From the outset of her reign she established herself as an energetic ruler, with a mind of her own and decided opinions as to what she wanted and how she would achieve it. She fostered Egyptian ways of life and paid great attention to religious practices. There is some evidence, not without dispute, that she travelled to Upper Egypt to attend the ceremony of the inauguration of the sacred bull Buchis at Hermonthis in March 51. Bulls were held in high esteem in many parts of Egypt, and worshipped as a living symbol of the gods. The citizens of Memphis honoured their own bull called Apis. When each animal died, a new one was installed in its place, the holy name was bestowed on it, and it was worshipped until it died. An inscription from Hermonthis indicates that Cleopatra, entitled the Queen, the Lady of the Two Lands (of Upper and Lower Egypt), rowed the sacred bull in the barge of Amon-Ra on the Nile. It has been suggested that this is all figurative, honouring Cleopatra in her absence, but there seems no reason to doubt that she went to the ceremony, expressing a personal interest in the well-being of her Egyptian subjects. This assiduous activity was appreciated by the people of Upper Egypt, who gave her sanctuary when she had been ejected from Alexandria by her brother, and in her last hour when she and Mark Antony were facing war with Octavian, the people declared themselves ready to rise up in arms to defend her. Her presence at this religious ceremony at Hermonthis, and perhaps at others elsewhere that have gone unrecorded by archaeological finds, need not be doubted.

She seems to have been reluctant at first to relinquish sole rule. For the first three years of her reign there is no mention of Ptolemy XIII, and then the papyrus sources indicate that the third year of Cleopatra's rule is also the first year of Ptolemy's. While exercising her sole power, she issued coins which displayed her head alone, an unprecedented move in a kingdom where Queens wielded considerable influence but definitely did not reign without a consort. It may be significant that Ptolemy XIII first appears as joint ruler only in troubled times. First of all there was a tense moment when Cleopatra faced potential trouble with Rome. In the aftermath of the disastrous defeat of Marcus Crassus by the Parthians in 53, Calpurnius Bibulus, the Roman governor of Syria, was threatened with retaliation by a Parthian invasion of his province in 51. In the end the invasion turned out to be less serious than he had imagined but as part of his preparations Bibulus decided to recall the Gabinian troops who had originally been part of the provincial troops in Syria. Accordingly he sent his two sons to Egypt to oversee the evacuation of the soldiers of Gabinius' army, but these men

3   Stele in the traditional antique Egyptian style from Hermonthis depicting the inauguration of the sacred bull, Buchis. Each time the bull died, a new animal was installed in place of the old one, with all appropriate religious observance. Cleopatra attended the ceremony of inauguration of the new Buchis on 22 March 51. Courtesy Ny Carlsberg Glyptotek

had settled down in Egypt and did not want to leave. They made their feelings abundantly clear when they murdered the two young men. At once, Cleopatra arrested the main culprits and despatched them to Bibulus, and fortunately the matter ended there. Bibulus acted with supreme correctness and sent the guilty men to be tried by the Senate in Rome. Apparently he did not hold Cleopatra responsible, or at least that was the public face he assumed. Privately he may have harboured a tremendous grudge against her, a small flame at first perhaps, fanned into conflagration by the company she kept after Pharsalus, when Bibulus' mortal enemy Julius Caesar took up residence with her in Alexandria.

The new Queen was probably relieved not to be held accountable for the murders of the two young Romans, nor was she charged with being unable to control her own army. At this moment she needed all the support she could muster, for internal problems beset her as well as external ones. Bad harvests in the autumn of 50 threatened famine and potential food riots. Cleopatra took immediate control of grain production, and decreed that all the produce of Middle Egypt must be transported to Alexandria and not, as was more usual, to Upper and Lower Egypt. Channelling food into Alexandria was a safeguard. The Alexandrians were a troublesome lot. They had killed Ptolemy XI, and had forced her father to leave the country, so she was not prepared to take any chances with them. As well as ensuring that their food supplies did not fail, perhaps it was only now, if she had not already done so, that she brought her younger brother to political prominence both to satisfy hallowed custom and put an end to suspicion that she intended to rule alone for ever. Perhaps more importantly, she no doubt knew that it was not only the Alexandrian population who might have been harbouring suspicions about her intentions. Rome was watching fairly closely, and it was known in Rome by the late summer of the previous year that her father was dead. It would also be common knowledge that Ptolemy XIII had not yet been acknowledged as colleague, and excuses about his extreme youth, or any other excuse she could advance for not promoting him, would be valid only for a limited duration.

There is another possible interpretation of the events of 50. As Michael Grant points out, the Royal decree forbidding transport of grain to Upper and Lower Egypt may indicate that it was Ptolemy and his courtiers who had the upper hand at that time, and the great quarrel between Cleopatra and her brother, noted by Caesar when he arrived in Egypt after Pharsalus, had already begun. The evidence will bear the interpretation that Ptolemy was in control of Alexandria, and Cleopatra was banished, so that the control of the food supply was not a prudent measure on her part to control the population of Alexandria, but an attempt by Ptolemy and his advisers to starve her out by removing food supplies from any part of the country, and also to prepare for a consequent siege of Alexandria by her armies. This quarrel was well advanced by the time that Caesar arrived in 48, but to project it backwards for two years may be stretching the evidence too far.

It is time to look at Cleopatra's origins and background, and her combined Macedonian and Egyptian heritage. One of the most surprising and tantalising mysteries about her is that no-one knows who was her mother, nor who was her grandmother, a lacuna in our knowledge that leads to all sorts of speculation. One suggestion is that Cleopatra was descended from a Syrian mother, whether a princess somehow secretly married to Auletes or a concubine. Neither theory is likely to be correct, but to dismiss a supposition does not help in establishing the truth. The charge of illegitimacy was apparently never made against Cleopatra, and it is surprising, if it were true, that her Roman enemies failed to use it. Another theory about Cleopatra's origins, is that her mother was of Ethiopian or African descent, and that she therefore combined Greek, Egyptian and African blood. The sources are too sparse to be certain, but no Roman source, and none of the surviving portraits of Cleopatra, lend any support at all to the theory that she may have been black. There was no colour prejudice in the twentieth-century sense in ancient Rome, but Octavian-Augustus would probably have made some mileage out of such information in his virulent propaganda against her. Proof or disproof of Cleopatra's true ancestry is impossible to find, so she is whatever people want her to be, and ultimately she would perhaps have been content with that aura of mystery.

From her father, Cleopatra inherited a prominent hooked nose, visible on her coin portraits, some of which are decidedly unflattering. Sculptural representations of her do not always show her with this pronounced nasal feature, but not all of the portraits of her are securely identified. Nevertheless those portraits which have gained general acceptance do not portray a woman of marked physical beauty. It was said by the ancient authors that Cleopatra was not beautiful in appearance, but her charming manner and her animated conversation,

4   *Coin portrait of*
      Cleopatra, showing
      her characteristic
      hairstyle, and her
      prominent hooked
      nose, inherited from
      her father. © British
      Museum

combined with her intelligence and education elevated her beyond the realm of physical perfection.

The kingdom that Cleopatra inherited was already old beyond reckoning, its administration very conservative, intensely regulated and centralised. The self-contained nature of Egypt made it easier to control, and the dependence of all the inhabitants upon the seasonal flooding of the Nile created mutual needs that positively demanded co-ordination by a central authority. The amalgam of Greek, Egyptian, Jewish and other elements worked better in Egypt than elsewhere because of this mutual dependence. There was already a substantial Greek population in Egypt even before the arrival of Alexander. The city of Naucratis was a Greek trading settlement tracing its origins back to a colonising venture of the seventh century. The other mainly Greek cities were Paraetonium, founded by Alexander on the western edge of the Delta, and Ptolemais founded by Ptolemy I Soter.

The greatest city of all was Alexandria, founded by Alexander in 332, and laid out on a grid plan by the Greek architect Dinocrates. Alexandria was a new city, built on the site of a village called Rhakotis, on the north western side of the Nile Delta. The planners took advantage of all the modern ideas that were current in the fourth century BC. The city was well defended, situated on a strip of land between the sea and Lake Mareotis, but the coast could be dangerous

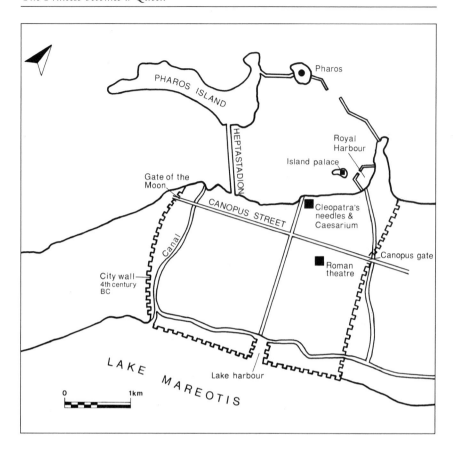

5 *Plan of Alexandria showing the main streets, the Pharos and the Royal Palace on a small island in the harbour. The city was protected on one side by the sea and on the other by Lake Mareotis. An earthquake destroyed most of the buildings on the waterfront in the fourth century. The famous lighthouse, the Pharos, one of the Seven Wonders of the World, finally disappeared in the fifteenth century. It stood on the western side of the great harbour, protected by the island named after it. The modern coastline now takes in the island, but in ancient times it was connected to the mainland only by the man-made causeway known as the Heptastadion. The submerged buildings in the harbour are currently under archaeological investigation, and many exciting finds have come to light. The ruins of the Pharos have been found, and recently a black granite sphinx was discovered, identified as a portrait of Ptolemy Auletes with his distinctive hooked nose. One of the most important finds is the magnificent ship, deliberately sunk in the Royal harbour. Archaeologists have suggested that it may be Cleopatra's Royal barge in which she sailed to meet Antony at Tarsus. Drawn by Graeme Stobbs*

for shipping until Ptolemy I Soter built the great lighthouse, or Pharos, on the little island off the shore — named Pharos island after the famous monument situated on it. There are many ancient representations of the Pharos, one of the Seven Wonders of the world, in paintings and mosaics, and on Roman coins. In 1997, underwater excavations conducted by French archaeologists revealed the foundations of the lighthouse, and investigations are still going on. The Pharos island and the mainland were connected by the Heptastadion, a man-made causeway, which provided a double harbour. Alexandria was always, and still is, in a class of its own and a law unto itself. Most modern capital cities of the world share this characteristic of a certain degree of difference and separateness from the rest of the country, largely because of their composite, international make-up, but in ancient Alexandria this separateness was taken somewhat further. People spoke of going from Alexandria to Egypt, a strange viewpoint to modern minds, akin to going from London to England or from Paris to France, which absurdity underlines the different ideology of the ancient Alexandrians. Their city was probably administered separately by the Ptolemies, and by the Romans, whose governors were described as prefects of Alexandria and Egypt.

Trade was Alexandria's raison d'être, and was conducted with the Mediterranean countries and with Africa and Ethiopia. The volume of trade was enhanced after Alexander destroyed the important city of Tyre, bringing Phoenician trading activities to a standstill. In 146 the Romans destroyed Carthage and also Corinth, and while the Alexandrians may have sympathised with the inhabitants of these cities, they were not averse to taking over any extra trade that came their way as a result. Dio of Prusa proclaimed that Alexandria controlled the trade of almost the whole world, and completely monopolised that of the Mediterranean. He may have exaggerated, but not by any marked degree.

Alexandria was probably the largest city in the ancient world, with a teeming ethnically mixed population. The main components of this population were the Egyptians, the Greeks, and a large proportion of Jews, who clustered mostly round the Royal Palace. Trouble occasionally flared up between these groups, and the population as a whole was always very near the flash point. Several of the Ptolemaic rulers had used force to keep the peace in Alexandria. It was a city of extremes; transient pleasures, decadence, and vice were ever present, but there was also the Museum, attached to the great and famous library, which drew scientists, poets and artists from all around the Mediterranean, creating the largest body of researchers and literati in the civilised world. There was a freedom of thought and expression in Alexandria which Rome never enjoyed.

The Greeks in Egypt did not follow the example of their ancestors, in that they did not form separate city states. The mountainous landscape in Greece itself, and the scattered islands of the wider Greek world, fostered this fragmented political development, because communications between cities were not easy and transport was better by sea than overland, so that the cities looked outwards to the Aegean and the Mediterranean rather than inward to any cohesive ideology of a single, united country. In Egypt, the opposite was true. The country looked in upon itself, and the landscape favoured cohesion. The Greek population blended reasonably well with the native Egyptians, not without occasional disputes, some of them fatal, but in general these problems were more domestic than national. The Alexandrians were more volatile and dangerous because of their numbers and co-ordination, and Cleopatra respected their power. Whenever possible she accommodated the Alexandrians, but mostly by manipulation rather than capitulation, by pre-empting trouble rather than waiting for it to happen and then meeting it head-on.

Cleopatra made a genuine effort to understand if not empathise with all the peoples in and around Egypt. She learned the native Egyptian language, the first of the Ptolemies to attempt to speak to her subjects in their own tongue. According to Plutarch, who wrote about her in his life of Mark Antony, she spoke several other languages as well as Greek and Egyptian, including Ethiopian, Hebrew, Aramaic, Syriac, Median and Parthian. These were the main and most important languages of the peoples around Egypt, with whom she would need to conduct diplomatic business or to arrange trading privileges. It may have been her father who encouraged her to learn these languages as part of a wider plan for Egypt. He encouraged, or at least did not discourage, trading contacts with the east via the Red Sea and the Indian Ocean, but his unfortunate reputation disallows him any credit for any far-seeing or co-ordinated policies. The inevitability of associating with Rome meant that all external policies and even purely national policies came under scrutiny whether or not Rome's 'friends and allies' (*amici*) acquiesced in such scrutiny, so if Cleopatra inherited any ideas from her father, she would have to subordinate them to the wishes of Rome. Acquiring languages could have been her own idea from the start. It may have been the case that she did not want to rely solely upon interpreters whenever she dealt with delegations or groups of people from other countries. These would not necessarily always be politically motivated encounters. She had a discerning financial sense, alert for any profitable venture, so more than ever she would need to know precisely what was being said. The closest modern analogy would be to imagine what it would be like to buy a used car in a country where one spoke none of the language.

Plutarch does not mention that Cleopatra spoke Latin, which seems to be a strange omission, since she spent most of her life dealing with Romans in one capacity or another. Perhaps it is to be taken as read that she spoke both Latin and Greek, and in any case, even if she spoke no Latin in her early youth, by the time she needed to speak to the leading Roman general of the day in 48, it is fairly certain that she would have acquired enough of the language to meet him on reasonable terms. If she spoke no Latin at all, then the conclusion is that all her conversations with Caesar, Antony and their friends were conducted in Greek. Most wealthy and educated Romans spoke Greek as a matter of course, and Cleopatra would deal only with the wealthy and educated classes, so it was perhaps not important to her to delve into the intricacies of perfect Latin or the dialects of Italy and the city of Rome.

By the third year of her reign Cleopatra was struggling not only for supremacy but also for existence. Her brother Ptolemy XIII and his advisers were increasingly hostile as they gained more influence, and at some unknown date Cleopatra fled to Upper Egypt, certainly deprived of power and perhaps even deposed by Ptolemy's council. The only account of this episode derives from the work of a Byzantine author, John Malalas, who wrote a history of the world from the Creation to the mid-sixth century. The source that he used is not known, but the story is probably true. Even if he made it all up, then it fits with the facts to be gleaned from the laconic account in Caesar's Civil War where it is merely stated that Ptolemy XIII had driven Cleopatra from the kingdom.

Her whereabouts are not known for certain until she came back to Alexandria in 48. It is probable that she travelled outside Egypt at some point at the end of 49 or the beginning of 48. Michael Grant suggests that she may have found refuge in Ascalon, a Philistine city which had ties with Egypt, having been supported by the Ptolemies against the aggressive intentions of the kings of Judaea. Presumably she had some kind of military force with her or she intended to raise an army to fight her way back into Egypt, which would require a great deal of time, effort and money. But before she had made much progress her prospects began to change; in August and September 48, events in Greece began to unfold that swept her along with them and finally secured her throne as Queen of Egypt.

From 49–8 the whole of the Roman world was involved in the power struggle between the two greatest generals, Caesar and Pompey, who had been heading towards civil war for several years. If Cleopatra had been in Rome with her father from 58–56 she would have met Pompey, since it was in his house in Rome that her father resided, and it was on Pompey that all her father's hopes were laid for restoration to his kingdom. She would also have heard of the proconsul Julius Caesar whose command in Gaul was proving so successful for Roman arms — at least by Caesar's own self-promoting accounts. Even if she had remained behind in Egypt while her father was absent, the association with Rome was so vital that she would no doubt have heard a great deal of these two political and military magnates, and their ally Marcus Licinius Crassus, who supplied much of the necessary cash to finance their political aims.

Although Caesar, Pompey and Crassus renewed their unofficial alliance in 56 at a conference at Luca in northern Italy, the foundations of their agreement began to crumble almost immediately. They had come together to satisfy their own individual needs, uniting to provide more coercive power to push through all the legislation that would bring them what they wanted, but they were never united in temperament or outlook. Pompey married Caesar's daughter Julia, and the short-lived marriage was a great success, but Julia died in childbirth in 54, and then in 53 Crassus was killed on campaign in Parthia, his dream of conquest shattered, and the eastern territories left unguarded and threatened. Whilst it can be argued that neither Julia nor Crassus provided any binding force in the political union, their deaths left two very powerful men facing each other without any real distractions or rivals.

The two generals had long ignored the conventions of Rome. Since there was no formal constitution as such in the government of Rome, it is spurious to speak of unconstitutional acts, but it is the only phrase that describes what was happening in Rome of the first century BC. In the old days, provincial commands were usually of fairly short duration, and likewise armies were temporary, raised to fight specific wars and then disbanded. But that had all begun to change from the days of Marius and Sulla and the civil wars of their generation. Provincial commands had become the real path to power, and the armies of Rome had evolved from state armies into much more personal armies loyal to their leaders. Dangerous precedents had been set, and Pompey and Caesar were alive to the possibilities.

For a while, civil war was avoided. Caesar renewed his proconsulship and remained in Gaul to complete his conquests, while Pompey stayed in Rome, governing his province of Spain through delegates, a hitherto unheard of arrangement. As proconsul of Spain in command of troops he was not technically supposed to set foot in Rome without first having laid down his command. Worse still, in 52 there was such unrest in the city that he was elected consul without a colleague, a tremendous anomaly in a city where consuls always came in pairs. Eventually he took his new father-in-law as colleague. Gradually he was drawn into the anti-Caesarean camp, and the road to civil war began with efforts to recall Caesar from his province. However Caesar had no intention of leaving until he was certain of the consulship immediately after his proconsulship. Proposals that both Caesar and Pompey should simultaneously lay down their commands were greeted with overwhelming popular support and just as overwhelmingly ignored by the factions in Roman politics.

When the civil war began, Pompey was not prepared, so he left Rome and then Italy, decamping for Greece, where he hoped to train and unite his army. Caesar was now free to do as he liked in Italy and Gaul, but he was flanked on east and west by Pompeian armies. Spain was held for Pompey by his faithful generals, Afranius and Petreius, and Greece was held by Pompey himself. Succinctly summing up the situation, Caesar decided to go to Spain first, saying he was going to fight an army without a general, then he would go to Greece to fight a general without an army. By the summer of 48 he was in Greece facing Pompey, and in August he defeated him at Pharsalus. Pompey escaped by the skin of his teeth, took ship and headed for Egypt, where his connections ought to have been secure enough to borrow money and raise another army. He had recently been made guardian of the young Ptolemy XIII, so he expected a friendly reception.

Ptolemy's advisers saw the matter differently. Close behind the defeated Pompey there would be the victorious Caesar. The war would continue on Egyptian soil with Egyptian supplies and Egyptian cash probably requisitioned for the purpose. The Romans seemed not to mind where they fought their battles or whose kingdoms they destroyed or annexed in the process. Pothinus, Ptolemy's councillor, and Achillas, his general, advised that Pompey should be eliminated, because as Achillas reputedly explained, dead men don't bite. Thus it was that when Caesar arrived in Alexandria he was presented with Pompey's head and his signet ring. The civil war was technically over, and the Alexandrians made it abundantly clear that they did not welcome the Roman consul or his display of Roman power. At that point, Caesar could have withdrawn from Egypt, but he chose to stay, sorting out internal Egyptian affairs on the pretext that he was collecting Auletes' debts, which he magnanimously reduced to half their value.

Cleopatra now re-entered the scene, as the story goes, carried in a rolled up carpet by her faithful follower Apollodorus, and laid at Caesar's feet. The tale has all the stuff of legend, but it may be true. Wherever she was when the news of Pharsalus reached her, followed by the news of Pompey's death and Caesar's arrival in Alexandria, Cleopatra would need to assess her situation very carefully. She was twenty-one years old, but experienced beyond her years, and very shrewd. She had no strong armies to use on her own account, and she would need help both to regain and retain her throne. The strongest source of help of any description in any part of the world at that moment was Caesar and his troops, and he was conveniently in Alexandria. This also meant that her brother Ptolemy XIII and his advisers now had immediate access to the Roman victor of Pharsalus, who might at any moment decide in Ptolemy's favour, swayed by the fact that it was in his name that Pompey had been so fortuitously removed from the scene, leaving Caesar blameless, exonerated and supreme in the Roman world. Next, there was the younger Ptolemy, aged about eleven, and their sister Arsinoe, perhaps about eighteen years old. These individuals may have possessed no personal aspiration to rule, but Arsinoe in particular had already revealed signs of great ambition, and even if she relinquished all claims to the throne, that was not the end of the matter. In the Royal Palace there would be many influential Macedonian Greeks and Egyptian officials whose interests

6   *Cartouche showing the name of Cleopatra in Egyptian hieroglyphics. Drawn by J.T. Taylor*

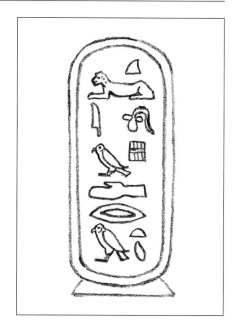

could be advanced by using either of the two Royal children as figureheads. Factional strife was not to be ruled out, and Caesar was the obvious source of arbitration and support. Allegedly she wrote to him stating her claims to the throne, but this was probably only a stopgap, in case she could not reach him herself. Letters were never reliable, for many reasons. Non-delivery was only one of the hazards; delivery to the wrong party was even worse, and even delivery to the correct party could still result in misunderstandings. It was essential therefore to get to Caesar before the others did, and to get to him in person and alone, not to his generals or to any of his assistants, and definitely not to any Egyptian or Greek official in Alexandria. Cleopatra probably did not trust anyone except her own immediate retinue. It was to Caesar that she must go to state her case, and she needed to do it directly and quickly. The rolled up carpet story is perfectly credible, and if it is not true it does not matter very much. Somehow, armed with nothing but confidence in herself and considerable personal charm, Cleopatra glided back into Alexandria, evading all potential opposition, and found Gaius Julius Caesar. She still had some problems to overcome, but from that moment on her throne was as secure as it could possibly be, and by the following year she was undoubted Queen of Egypt.

2. Caesar

The Alexandrians objected to Caesar's presence even more strongly when they began to suspect that he intended to make Cleopatra Queen. From their point of view it was irritating enough that she would be their ruler, but what was even more galling was the fact that she was so resolute and single-minded, not subject to influence or coercion, and it seemed that Caesar would support her as sole ruler, without a consort. Reviewing the four surviving heirs to the Egyptian throne, Caesar had to make decisions as to their fate. He had already summoned Ptolemy XIII to the Royal Palace, and whether he summoned her or not, Cleopatra arrived. Arsinoe was also residing in the Palace, as was the younger Ptolemy. Each would have their own staff and courtiers, so the potential for intrigue was vastly increased.

Some effort at reconciliation between Cleopatra and Ptolemy XIII had to be made, with Caesar's backing. Other than trying to put into effect a settlement of the Royal household, Caesar had no solid excuse to remain in Egypt, and at this point he could have withdrawn, but past experience had proved that Rome and Egypt had mutual needs which would be compromised if Caesar simply turned his back and left the various factions to fight it out. Any other Roman general in the same position would have stayed to settle the question of the succession to the throne of Auletes, though in this particular instance we can only conjecture what was the content of the interviews, conversations and finally pillow talk between Caesar and Cleopatra.

They both had extremely strong interests in control of Egypt. From Cleopatra's point of view there could be no compromise. Either she ruled, and ruled unopposed, or she was as good as dead, so in seeking for support from Caesar she risked everything. If he refused her, favouring Ptolemy XIII and his motley crew, she had nowhere else to turn. It was clear that Ptolemy, accompanied by Pothinus and Achillas, would soon marginalise her or even eliminate her. Therefore she required support, preferably armed support, until she was properly established, and Caesar was both on the spot and tolerably well armed. From the Roman point of view, peace in Egypt was a priority, not from any humanitarian considerations, but purely from the selfish Roman outlook. A weakened Egypt preoccupied with fighting civil wars did not constitute a direct threat, but such a series of events would also weaken and perhaps destroy the source of wealth that could be siphoned off for Rome, and much worse, allies from other eastern countries might be called in to fight on behalf of one of the factions, and thereby gain a foothold in the country — and Rome ought to know all about how that was done because she was adept at it herself. If any of the eastern kings or petty princes followed the example of the first Ptolemy and made Egypt into a private kingdom, then Rome would have to tread very carefully, so it was better to avert that possibility before it happened.

Naturally, Caesar was not as altruistic as all that; personal interests entered into the picture as well as wider political concerns. There would be tremendous advantages for him personally if he could keep the ruler or rulers of Egypt grateful to him for their thrones, and therefore under his thumb. The importance of Egypt as a personal preserve was considerable, as revealed some years before by Pompey's interest in the matter, and again some years later by Octavian's treatment of the country after the battle of Actium. The way in which he administered it was a departure from normal practice. He placed the province under an equestrian, not a senatorial, governor and he never relinquished his control of it to the Senate. When he was established as head of state with the honorary title of Augustus, he restored to the Senate some of its powers and the administration of some of the less important provinces, but just as he retained control of all the major provinces with armies, he did not relinquish Egypt, even forbidding senators to enter the country without express permission. Caesar would not be blind to all these considerations when he first heard Cleopatra's story.

Matters soon came to a head. Caesar and Cleopatra, famously, must have become lovers very soon after their first meeting. It may have been a part of Cleopatra's strategy to captivate the Roman general in order to win him to her cause, or it may have been part of Caesar's plans to charm Cleopatra and make her more compliant. On the other

7   *Head of Gaius Julius Caesar, the victor of Pharsalus, who followed Pompey to
Alexandria. According to the terms of Ptolemy Auletes' will, his son Ptolemy and
his daughter Cleopatra were to be joint rulers after his death. Caesar eventually
found in favour of Cleopatra alone, installing her as Queen of Egypt.
Courtesy Vatican Museums, Vatican City*

hand, political motives may have been swept aside by simple biological urges. Caesar was in his fifties, married more than once, experienced, charismatic, and a known womaniser. Cleopatra was twenty-two, not classically beautiful but extremely attractive, and perhaps almost as experienced as Caesar in the ways of the world. She had grown up in a hard and violent milieu, but whatever cynicism she might have developed did not overwhelm her. She was engaging and clever, and Caesar liked women who were clever. But it is unlikely that both participants lost their heads. They were both of them too shrewd, too self-controlled and too aware not only of their immediate needs but also the long-term consequences of what they did. They probably discussed the ground rules under a series of main headings and sub-clauses before they went to bed.

When he realised that his sister had already found more than just favour with Caesar, Ptolemy staged a public tantrum, stirring up the population of Alexandria on the basis that he was being displaced by Cleopatra. Caesar issued benign statements, followed by a cosmetic celebration of the joint rule of Ptolemy XIII and Cleopatra, with feasting and festivities that probably sounded very hollow. There remained the two siblings, Arsinoe and the younger Ptolemy. In settling their fortunes, Caesar hoped to reconcile both the Alexandrians and the Egyptians by setting up the two remaining Ptolemies as independent rulers of Cyprus. This was a bold move. The island had only recently been wrenched from Ptolemaic control and arbitrarily annexed by Rome, and the stern Marcus Porcius Cato had been sent out as its first governor. The correct procedure should have involved the Senate in debate about returning Cyprus to the Ptolemies, but Caesar had already revealed his lack of respect for this long-winded approach, and did not feel the need for seeking senatorial permission. Besides he had to do something rapidly to assuage the volatile population of Alexandria and to try to avert Palace rebellions in the name of any of the four Ptolemaic heirs. In Alexandria he had to be seen to be trying hard to pour oil on troubled waters. If the Senate objected then he could always deal with the situation later when he returned to Rome.

The settlements were precarious at best and the balance could be easily upset. The political jostling was exacerbated by Pothinus, one of the most prominent members of Ptolemy XIII's entourage and his most influential and ambitious adviser. It probably seemed to him an

8 *Head of Cleopatra as a young woman. Her features are not portrayed in idealistic fashion, which suggests that the sculptor did not flatter her and perhaps captured something of her true appearance. Though not classically beautiful, she was very attractive, and besides her physical appearance she emanated fascination and charm in her speech and manner. She was only 22 years old when she first met Caesar and claimed her throne with his support. © British Museum*

ideal situation that all the main protagonists were contained in one place, while Ptolemy's army was intact outside Alexandria. Accordingly he sent a message to Achillas, in command of the army, to bring the troops to Alexandria and put the Royal Palace under siege. Pothinus was determined to place Ptolemy XIII firmly on the throne, with himself as chief adviser, courtier and councillor, and it would not matter to him who was the Royal consort, provided that it was not Cleopatra. If the siege succeeded he could remove at one stroke the Romans and all the opponents of his schemes. Accidents could happen to anyone during sieges; Cleopatra, Arsinoe and the young Ptolemy could all conveniently disappear. It is even possible that Pothinus had thought ahead about what to do with Caesar, perhaps counting on the enormous wealth that would be at his disposal with which to bribe his way into power if Caesar survived. Hardened ascetic though he was, Caesar was still very interested in money for the power that it brought in its wake, so Pothinus perhaps construed the situation as cut and dried, imagining that Caesar could be easily bought off, if it proved impossible to kill him. More realistically, he probably determined at the outset to have Caesar killed, counting on the fact that the Roman Senate might actually be grateful if he removed Caesar, since he would know that the two of them were never the best of friends.

Achillas duly brought up the army and placed the Royal Palace under siege. Caesar was now at a grave disadvantage, outnumbered and enclosed. He could not simply walk out of the Palace and then the city, and access to the sea was denied, so escape was impossible, unless he could neutralise the Egyptian fleet. This was his first priority, and in a surprise attack he captured the fleet and burned the ships before Pothinus or Achillas could use them against him. The details of how this was achieved are obscure. There may have been some tense moments with Caesar as spectator or participant, but in his description of these events in his *Civil War*, Caesar does not elaborate. While the ships burned the fire spread to the city, and it is widely believed that the great library of Alexandria went up in flames. This tale may have been a result of Egyptian propaganda, to illustrate how the barbarous Roman general paid no heed to what he destroyed as long as he got his own way. Something of the sort may actually have happened, but in the *Alexandrian War* Aulus Hirtius, possibly using Caesar's notes, reported that the buildings of Alexandria were almost fireproof, because they were all built using an arched construction and contained no wooden joinery. Timber was not abundant, imports were costly, and building techniques accommodated the needs of the population and suited the climate. Hirtius' statement may have been a veiled apology for the calamity, but it is unlikely that the entire library was burned. It is an enduring legend, and made good copy both at the time and down the ages.

If Achillas had acted quickly he could have recouped some of his losses by seizing the famous lighthouse, the Pharos, at the harbour mouth. If he had been able to do this, the advantage that Caesar had just gained in destroying the fleet would have been invalidated, since even without enemy ships to oppose him, he would not have been able to pass the Pharos unscathed, and therefore would still have been unable to escape via the sea, nor would he have been able to bring in reinforcements, or supplies. Consequently, without pausing after the capture of the fleet, Caesar acted with characteristic dash and seized the Pharos himself, splendidly consolidating his victory. The first round had thus been won by Caesar. Now everything depended on the siege of the Royal Palace. Cleopatra will have observed events with keen interest. Now that events had taken such a desperate turn, there could be little chance of a negotiated peace. If Caesar failed, she failed. Their futures were already interlocked.

All that Caesar could do for the time being was to create defences around the Palace, and fight off attacks. He was still outnumbered, and from the autumn to the winter of 48, that was how it remained. Then the antagonisms between the Ptolemies and their rival factions played into his hands. Arsinoe fled to Achillas, perhaps hoping to persuade him to make her Queen, as consort to either of her brothers. She took with her one of her courtiers, Ganymedes, which turned out disastrously because he and Achillas instantly fell out. Their quarrel spread to their retinues and then to the army, with the result that each faction vied for control of it, bribing their way into command. Caesar no doubt quietly rejoiced at the disintegration of unity in the Ptolemaic army. He chose this moment to execute Pothinus for stirring up trouble and communicating with Achillas. It was not a sudden whim; Pothinus had always been a dangerous liability. Caesar later proclaimed that Pothinus would have killed him if he had not executed him first. All the time acting correctly, Caesar was probably merely awaiting the perfect opportunity, and there would never be a better one. Very gradually, the opposition to Cleopatra and Caesar was being eliminated.

Arsinoe had shown her hand but not yet won the victory, and now Pothinus was dead.

Without Pothinus to provide him with information, and beset by internal squabbles, Achillas found everything unravelling all around him, and was soon murdered by or on the orders of Ganymedes, who took command of the army. For a while the new commander fought intelligently and aggressively against Caesar, first trying to cut off his supplies of fresh water by letting the sea into the sweet water of Lake Mareotis. The Roman soldiers dug wells as fast as Ganymedes spoiled the water supply but Caesar knew that this could not go on indefinitely. Fortunately Ganymedes' days were numbered because Roman reinforcements were sailing towards Alexandria. They arrived in December. This meant that Ganymedes had to face two contingents of Caesar's troops, and he was without a fleet, but his situation was not as disadvantageous as it sounds and there was still some hard fighting. Though he had captured the lighthouse at the harbour mouth, Caesar did not yet have full control of the island on which the lighthouse was built. Consequently he was not in complete command of the entire bay, and in trying to fortify the causeway along the western side of the harbour between the Pharos island and the Alexandrian mainland, he nearly lost his life. He ferried troops to the island on board ship, captured it and destroyed the buildings, and next day began to erect a rampart on the causeway connecting the island to the mainland. While the ramparts were being built up, the Egyptians attacked from the landward side and from the sea. The Roman ships drew off, everyone panicked because they thought they were about to be abandoned, too many men tried to board too few ships, which started to sink. Caesar quickly realised that his own ship would capsize, so he dived into the water and swam for safety. This is the laconic version of the *Alexandrian War* but Plutarch adds the details that Caesar swam with one hand while holding a bundle of papers, presumably papyrus sheets, above his head to keep them dry. Caesar left his purple cloak behind which the enemy declared was a trophy, as though he was either vain enough or foolish enough to try to swim while wearing it, and had somehow lost it in transit.

After more skirmishing of this sort, with little hope of a quick victory for either side, the Alexandrians petitioned Caesar to let Ptolemy XIII return to them. The envoys told him that Ganymedes was too tyrannical, and that being tired of war they would make a pact with

Caesar if Ptolemy ordered it. There was some play-acting and crocodile tears as Ptolemy left, but once with his army he revealed that he also had crocodile teeth, and renewed hostilities with great determination. The time for the final battle was approaching. At the beginning of the siege Caesar had sent his ally Mithridates of Pergamum to Syria and Cilicia to round up reinforcements. Mithridates was an important and wealthy individual who had been adopted by king Mithridates the Great, from whom he took his name, one which carried a great deal of influence. He had collected a considerable army with which he now besieged Pelusium, situated east of Alexandria, guarding the approach overland from Syria. It was occupied by a garrison placed there by Achillas, but Mithridates soon overcame resistance and appeared at the Delta, where Ptolemy tried to stop him. Seizing his chance, Caesar left Alexandria and came up behind Ptolemy's army. The events of the battle of the Nile, fought in March 47, are recounted in the *Alexandrian War*; the result was that Ptolemy XIII was drowned in the Nile, and resistance was at an end, but not before Caesar ordered a search for the body of the king to prove that Ptolemy was dead and therefore mortal. The Egyptians believed that drowning in the Nile, so inextricably connected with the Osiris legend, conferred instant deification. Ptolemy as a living person had been problematic enough, but Ptolemy as a dead king converted into a living god would have been a very great obstacle for Cleopatra to overcome. Caesar would be aware of the legends, but it was probably Cleopatra who best understood the deep significance that her countrymen would attach to it, and probably she who persuaded Caesar to put an end to all doubts about Ptolemy's fate.

In the *Alexandrian War* there is no mention of Cleopatra throughout all these events, except for an almost casual note in chapter 33 describing how Caesar made himself master of Egypt and Alexandria (note the separate description of the country and then the city), and then appointed rulers as outlined in Auletes' will. Since the elder Ptolemy was dead, the kingdom was assigned to the younger Ptolemy, now Ptolemy XIV, and his sister Cleopatra, 'who had remained loyal' to Caesar. This small statement speaks volumes for their political and personal relationship throughout the Alexandrian war. It is most likely Caesar's own comment, either in note form or possibly an oral statement. Whoever was the ultimate author of the *Alexandrian War*, no matter if it was, or was not, Aulus Hirtius, he could have found a way of avoiding any comment at all on Cleopatra's loyalties. It is implied that she had remained in the theatre of war, with Caesar and the troops, and whilst it might be argued that in the siege of the Palace she had no choice, it is also a tribute to her personal courage and her steadfast adherence to her own and Caesar's cause.

Cleopatra had reached the pinnacle of success. She was Queen of Egypt, with the support of the most powerful general in the Roman world, thereby connected to everything that the nascent Roman Empire had to offer, and virtually unencumbered with rivals at home. Her consort, symbolically her husband in accordance with Egyptian regal practice, was her twelve year old brother Ptolemy XIV. Strictly he was her half-brother, since they did not share the same mother. He does not feature very prominently in the administration of the kingdom, which implies that he was useful for ceremonial but really only retained for cosmetic purposes to mollify the population. Having witnessed what happened to ambitious members of the Ptolemaic Royal family, perhaps he did not entertain high-flying aspirations, content to remain in the background. More importantly it seems that there were no politically ambitious personnel around him who wished to agitate on his behalf. Cleopatra's only surviving rival was her sister Arsinoe, who was declared a traitor and sent as a prisoner to Rome, where some time later she would appear in Caesar's triumph, led through the streets to the Capitol as a captive princess. The island of Cyprus, briefly granted to Arsinoe and Ptolemy XIII as independent rulers, was instead restored to the kingdom of Egypt under Cleopatra and Ptolemy XIV.

Both Caesar and Cleopatra now had what they wanted. Egypt had escaped formal annexation and conversion into a Roman province. That would come later when Octavian appropriated the country and its wealth. It suited Caesar's purpose not to annexe the country, and it is certain that Caesar was the driving force behind the treatment of Egypt, no matter how captivated he may have been with Cleopatra, nor how persuasive she was in angling for what she needed. Cleopatra retained her position by a fortuitous combination of circumstances, for however much she charmed Caesar and however much he may have loved her, Caesar's political ideology always ruled whatever he did. Emotions came low down on his list of political priorities. If he detested Cleopatra but considered her a useful ally and capable of ruling Egypt without endangering him or the nascent Roman Empire, he would still have installed her as Queen; if he loved her but considered her incompetent and unsatisfactory, he would have made alternative arrangements, retaining as far as possible his influence over the chosen ruler or rulers. He avoided formal annexation because it would have removed Egypt from his control and placed it under the Senate, unless of course he chose to do as Octavian did in 30, categorically denying to the senators the remotest interest in the province, and for that, Caesar was not yet secure enough. He chose to leave Egypt independent under its rightful Queen, over whom it is to be supposed that he had some personal influence, so he had the best of both worlds.

His only alternative apart from these semi-private arrangements would have been to convert Egypt into a province and try to ensure that he governed it himself via legates, as Pompey governed Spain. However the Romans had seen through that kind of scheme by now and would not countenance it without a struggle. Caesar adopted a diluted form of this sort of government, leaving troops behind when he left Egypt under an officer called Rufio, who had risen from the ranks, and who had every reason to be loyal to Caesar for his advancement. The motive for lending armed support to Cleopatra was double-edged. She needed to keep the population of Alexandria under control, and to weed out undesirable elements in her court so that she could establish complete authority over her entourage. Rufio was no doubt a good officer and respectful to Cleopatra, and he and his troops would help her to maintain control, but he would also keep Caesar informed of what developments took place in Egypt. If Cleopatra began to show dissident tendencies — dissident that is from Caesar's world-view — then there would be a means of curbing her. It would be so interesting to know what was Rufio's brief when Caesar put him in command of the contingents left in Egypt.

There is the question of how far Caesar and Cleopatra trusted one another. For the time being they were in accord about Egypt's future and its place in the Roman world, but times could change. It is certain that just as Caesar would have been totally ruthless about how he dealt with both Egypt and Cleopatra, then vice versa if circumstances changed, Cleopatra would put the interests of Egypt before her private feelings for Caesar as a man and her political perceptions of him as a Roman ally. In the event, Caesar had only three more years to live before he was assassinated, and their political relationship was never seriously tested, nor does it seem that they were ever at odds with each other in their private lives. But even if they did trust each other to any degree, their trust would have always been tempered with stark realism.

In order to underscore their current association, and perhaps also for pleasure and diversion, when the battles were over and Cleopatra was firmly established as Queen, Caesar accompanied her on a grand tour up the Nile. Presumably Caesar attached tremendous importance to this leisurely cruise, since there were many problems facing him in more than one part of the Roman world. Some of Pompey's adherents were entrenched in Africa, preparing to continue the civil war and gaining strength every day. One of Caesar's lieutenants, Domitius Calvinus, left in charge of the province of Asia, was embroiled in a struggle against Pharnaces, king of Pontus, who laid claim to Lesser Armenia and Cappadocia, hoping to gain a foothold while the Romans were pre-occupied in fighting each other. There was much for Caesar to attend to, not least in Rome itself, but he stayed in Egypt apparently enjoying himself. The evidence will bear that interpretation, especially since there is very little of it with which to refute the charge, but it is highly unlikely that there was no political motive behind Caesar's Nile cruise.

For Cleopatra, it was highly important. She had already demonstrated that she was more than superficially concerned with the welfare of the Egyptian population as well as the Macedonian and Greek inhabitants. The Nile journey would serve several purposes, to create a sense of unity among the entire kingdom, to show herself to the people as no Ptolemy had ever done before, communicating with them on many levels, open and accessible, but never forgetting that she was all-powerful, all-seeing, all-knowing, and that moreover Roman support in the form of Julius Caesar was never far behind her. It was a fortunate blend of Royal progress, diplomatic mission and show of strength.

When the cruise ended with the return to Alexandria, Caesar finally left Egypt, at some time in mid-summer. Despite various suggestions, both ancient and modern, no-one knows the precise date when he took his leave, nor when he arrived in Syria to begin the short campaign against Pharnaces. Cleopatra was heavily pregnant by now, giving birth shortly after Caesar departed, to her son nicknamed by the Alexandrians as little Caesar, or Caesarion. His official name given to him by Cleopatra was Ptolemy Caesar, indicating his combined Egyptian and Roman origins. These origins and even the date of birth

9   *Relief portraits of Cleopatra and her son Caesarion in the antique Egyptian*
     tradition, from the wall of the temple at Dendera in Upper Egypt. As ruler of Egypt
     Cleopatra adopted the traditional Pharaonic regal and religious symbolism, taking
     care to include Caesarion in her iconography. Here they are depicted as Isis and
     Horus, the mother and son of the Osiris-Isis-Horus legend. Photo David Brearley

have been doubted, dismissed and discussed from Cleopatra's times to the present day, without much hope of any possibility of final resolution.

Caesarion's true paternity is not so important as his political status. Cleopatra intended that Egypt and the world should recognise the boy not only as Caesar's son, but also the heir to the throne of the Ptolemies. She promoted him as such all through his short life, sharing the throne with him after the death of her brother, when Caesarion was only three years old. She was obviously tutoring him for the succession, spreading the same consistent message to the Romans and the Mediterranean world in one direction and to the native Egyptians and the tribes beyond Egypt in the other. Caesarion is depicted as Pharaoh with his mother on the famous reliefs on the outer wall of the temple at Dendera in Upper Egypt. Perhaps more eloquent for the Egyptians was the depiction at the shrine at Hermonthis, where the birth of Caesarion to Cleopatra is unmistakably equated with Isis giving birth to Horus, which placed the rulers in a divine context as Pharaohs and gods. Cleopatra played her part with skill and understanding, taking her example from previous Ptolemies who cultivated the loyalty of the Egyptians in the old accustomed manner.

It is equally significant that Caesar is said to have acknowledged Caesarion as his son. The source for this is not Caesar's writings or anything directly associated with him; it derives from the life of Caesar by Suetonius, who tells us that in a speech to the Senate Mark Antony testified that Caesar had acknowledged Caesarion in front of witnesses, notably his friend Gaius Matius and his secretaries Oppius and Balbus. This public acknowledgement is most likely true. After that it did not matter whether Caesar really was the father of the child or not. Both he and Cleopatra made a declaration to the world and did not care whether the world chose to believe it or not. Alternative versions would be current as soon as the boy was born, including the possibility that Cleopatra had taken a lover and passed off his offspring as Caesar's, or more preposterously that the twelve year old Ptolemy was the father of Cleopatra's son. One man who did take the alleged paternity of the young Caesarion extremely seriously was Octavian, Caesar's great nephew and son by adoption. He knew only too well that there could be no rivals for Caesar's heritage, so Caesarion, whether the true son or otherwise of Caesar, had to be eliminated.

Cleopatra honoured Caesar, and underlined her association with him, by building the Caesareum, a huge edifice with colonnades, high enough to be visible to sailors as they came into the harbour. Two obelisks, already ancient by Cleopatra's day, but now commonly called Cleopatra's needles, stood outside this building. One of these 'needles', the obelisk of Thutmosis III, is now situated on the Thames embankment in London, England. Keeping Caesar's memory alive in Egypt emphasised his importance, and paved the way for their son Caesarion to fulfil his intended role as descendant of the Ptolemies, supported by Rome. When Caesar left, Cleopatra could not be sure that she would ever see him again, so she could not rely upon his continued presence or even long-standing influence in Egyptian affairs. She had to make the best of the situation as it stood, and be prepared to meet all challenges alone.

In the event, she was not parted from Caesar for very long. His victory over Pharnaces was soon won, so soon in fact that Caesar summed it up himself in a succinct and well-known phrase *veni, vidi, vici*, 'I came, I saw, I conquered'. But this was only one of several wars that he would have to wage. The last of the Pompeian armies were not yet eradicated. As has been mentioned, there was a growing resistance in north Africa, where several of Pompey's officers and men had found refuge after Pharsalus. They had had time to recruit others to their cause, such as king Juba of Mauretania, whose resources were not negligible. It may have made military sense to sail directly to Africa after the successful conclusion of the war against Pharnaces, but Caesar had not seen Rome for nearly two years, and trouble was brewing, both politically and economically. In late summer 47, he arrived home to find that no elections had been held to choose magistrates for the following year, debt was rife, there had been extensive rioting, and his lieutenants Mark Antony and Dolabella had been unable to contain it. On the contrary, Dolabella agitated on behalf of debtors, Antony did nothing for a while and when he did finally act and successfully stopped the riots he was accused of being too brutal. Caesar dropped him for a while. He had other problems. Even his own troops were disaffected, being unwilling to embark on Caesar's next campaign; Africa was a long way away and they were tired. Caesar quelled a near mutiny by appearing before the soldiers in person and addressing them not as fellow soldiers (*commilitones*) but as fellow citizens (*quirites*), indicating that he would dismiss them all and go to fight in Africa without them. Naturally they then wanted to follow him wherever he took them. The Senate and people of Rome acquiesced in the choice of Marcus Aemilius Lepidus and Caesar as the consuls for 46, and whatever magistrates who had Caesar's backing were elected for the other posts. Few people were in any position to disagree.

At the end of 47 Caesar set off for Africa, travelling via Sicily. The African war ended with the battle of Thapsus on 6 April 46; the whole campaign is described by an unknown author, one of Caesar's associates, who may also have written the account of the Spanish war. It is argued that these two works differ in style from that of the *Alexandrian War*, and that therefore Aulus Hirtius, widely accepted as the author of the latter, was not the author of the *African War*. The information contained in the account most probably derived from Caesar's own notes. Cleopatra will have heard of his success, perhaps even via messages from Caesar himself. She may also have heard that he had been more than diplomatically friendly with the wife of Bogud, king of Mauretania. The rumours may not have bothered her very much. She probably realised from the start that she could not settle down with Caesar in conjugal bliss and perpetual domestic nonentity. He was already married to Calpurnia, and by Roman law he was not allowed to marry a foreigner. Besides, they were both quite removed from the mundane spheres of the merely ordinary, and she had obtained most of what she wanted for the time being, support for her regime and a son by Caesar himself. The wife of king Bogud had not achieved such heights.

Caesar returned to Rome in September 46, where he celebrated four belated triumphs, over Gaul, Egypt, Pontus, and Africa. Victory over individuals was not mentioned, nor was it pointed out too clearly that the African victory was over fellow Romans. In the Egyptian triumph, Cleopatra's half sister Arsinoe was led through Rome, but spared the usual death by strangling that normally awaited conquered leaders of Rome's enemies. Instead she was packed off to Asia Minor to find sanctuary at the temple of Artemis at Ephesus, at least for a while. Her ultimate fate was to be executed on the orders of Antony and Cleopatra, when she was suspected of agitating against them.

At some time in 46, Cleopatra and her son came to Rome. She made the journey for several reasons, not least because she probably wanted to see Caesar again. She was fond of him, if not in love with him, and it is not recorded that she took any other lovers in his absence. In

10 *Head of Cleopatra from Alexandria, very worn, but with features which support
the identification as a portrait of the Queen. Graeco-Roman Museum, Alexandria,
Egypt. Photo David Brearley*

addition she required official recognition for the status of her country and her own person vis a vis Rome. It is usually assumed that Caesar's arrangements with her, whatever they were, would have to be ratified by the Senate, designating Cleopatra a friend of the Roman people. This was an official phrase, applied to cities, states and individuals alike. The agreement was entered into and terminated according to a formal procedure, but this did not necessarily involve a formal treaty, unless each party entered into an alliance which would then go beyond the loose, unofficial association of friendship (*amicitia*), by defining certain legal obligations on both sides, often with an imbalance in Rome's favour. Cleopatra certainly did not want to become merely a Roman puppet, but on the other hand she was a hard-headed realist, and knew that she could not hope to stand alone in the world. At present her country was stable thanks to Caesar, but her association with him was not enough. While he was strong and had access to armed support it was sufficient, but Cleopatra no doubt reasoned that Caesar may not always be in such a supreme position. He was not young, and would certainly not live for ever. He might die or be killed in battle before Cleopatra had fully established herself, and even if he did not die, Roman politicians lost power as quickly as they gained it, and with Caesar removed from the scene and no other friendly Roman contacts, Cleopatra and Egypt would be at the mercy of whichever predatory Roman general emerged from the next round of political bargaining or even civil wars. She had impressed Caesar. Now she needed to impress Rome, to ensure her survival beyond Caesar.

It was not just a matter of personal survival, or a selfish desire for self-aggrandisement. Those who have questioned Cleopatra's motives in this respect are short-sighted. When she became Queen of Egypt, Cleopatra took on the permanent task of ruling her country, keeping it intact, and providing for its inhabitants, and this task had to be done properly or not at all. It mean that her personal life and political life were so smoothly blended that there was no distinction between them. Only very rarely would there be any free moments when Cleopatra could forget that she had a role to fulfil and was playing the part of the Queen. She took it seriously and played it well. Cleopatra was Egypt, and the welfare of Egypt depended on her continued survival.

In Rome she may have allowed herself to relax occasionally, but there was always the matter of Egypt and its status with regard to

Rome. Cleopatra wanted a formal treaty signed and sealed by recognised Roman representatives and brought before the Senate for ratification. She probably also intended to form as many business and financial contacts as she could. According to Dio, writing in the third century, a treaty was arranged, but the exact terms of it are not known, nor is it known on which source Dio based this story. There is no reason to doubt that some such arrangements were made. It is not too fanciful to imagine Caesar and Cleopatra going through the relevant documents, weighing words until all the main provisions were catered for and all the loose ends were neatly tied up. Perhaps Caesar read it to a submissive Senate who put up no argument; if there had been any serious trouble, Caesar's enemies would no doubt have recorded it, and Octavian would have made use of the events to blacken the names of Cleopatra and Antony when the time came to prepare for war against them.

There is some argument as to whether Cleopatra was present in Rome for Caesar's triumphs, and consequently able to see Arsinoe led through the streets behind Caesar's chariot. There are those apologists who suggest that it would not have been politic for her to be present at a triumph over her own country, therefore she could not have seen her sister's degradation, and yet others who insist that it must have been owing to her influence that Arsinoe was allowed to go free. On the other hand there is a case for her presence at the Egyptian triumph to enable her to demonstrate her detachment from the events of the Alexandrian war, in which she was decidedly in Caesar's camp. The victory was over Ptolemy XIII, and his advisers Pothinus and Achillas, not over the Queen.

During her stay in Rome, Cleopatra stayed for some of the time in Caesar's house across the Tiber. Cicero refers to her stay there in one of his letters to Atticus, written after the assassination of Caesar, when he felt free to express his dislike of the Queen. He mentions her arrogance and the insolence of her staff, chiefly concerned of course with the detrimental effect on himself. Perhaps he and Cleopatra had already met when Auletes was in Rome, in which case he could perhaps not reconcile himself to the changes in their relative positions. In 58 he had been forced into exile by the rabble-rouser Publius Clodius, who as tribune of the plebs revived the law that execution of citizens without trial was punishable by banishment. This was aimed directly at Cicero, whose finest hour had been achieved when he was

11 *Marcus Tullius Cicero, author of the Philippics, orations directed against Mark*
Antony after the assassination of Caesar. Cicero wrote about Cleopatra to his friend
Atticus on a few occasions, referring to her as the Queen. He found her arrogant
and in one letter he said that he hated her.
Photo courtesy of the Victoria and Albert Museum

consul in 63, unmasking the conspiracy of Catiline but acting hastily in having the conspirators condemned to death without risking the formality and possible delays of a trial. After a short and very miserable period away from Rome he was recalled in August 57 at the instigation of his friend Pompey, so when he arrived home in September 57 his head would be fuller than ever of his own importance and no doubt flooded with relief. He would have scarcely noticed Auletes the ruler of Egypt and his very young daughter, and if he did enquire after them he would dismiss them as hapless individuals who were in desperate need of help and were completely in Pompey's pocket. A decade later in 46 Cleopatra was Queen of Egypt and had a clearly defined sense of her own importance and abilities. She could readily identify those people who were useful to her, those who were to be respected, those to be feared and those who counted for very little. With Caesar at her elbow this sifting of personnel would be much easier. Cicero's fame was not as brilliant as it had been, and though Caesar may have respected him, listened to him and on occasion even taken his advice, for the most part he by-passed him when it came to important decisions. Cleopatra would take her cue from Caesar, and Cicero would not like it at all. Apparently she promised him some gifts of a literary nature, which Cicero said he would not be ashamed to announce in the Senate (in case it should be thought that he had accepted bribes), but he was piqued because he had not received them. All in all the association was not a happy one, though Cicero was the most voluble about it; Cleopatra probably never gave him a second thought. She was on a different plane.

Other eminent Romans would have been introduced to her while she was in Rome, and would perhaps have been very eager to meet her, simply to inspect her and to fawn on one of Caesar's associates. She may have met Mark Antony again, remembering all that he had done to restore Auletes to the throne while at the same time avoiding a bloodbath of revenge just after the restoration. She may have liked him, and the feelings may have been reciprocated, but Antony had just married the current love of his life, Fulvia, whose previous two husbands, both deceased, had been the friends of his youth, Clodius and Curio. Mark Antony was probably too preoccupied to pay much attention to Cleopatra, and if he had gone too far in trying to get to know her he may have jeopardised his friendship with Caesar, to whose mast Antony had irrevocably nailed his colours.

Of all the entourage surrounding Caesar, perhaps the most inconsequential at this time was his great nephew Gaius Octavius, still a teenager, frail, always ill, but with an understanding quite beyond his years and possessed of an iron determination and fortitude totally belied by his appearance. Caesar had already noticed him, and begun to promote him, but at this stage it did not seem so significant as it would a short time later. When Caesar left Rome in 46 for Spain, it was intended that Octavius should accompany him, but once again the youth was ill. Undeterred, when he recovered he set off with a few friends and arrived at Caesar's camp just too late for the final battle at Munda. He had demonstrated many of the qualities that Caesar liked, overcoming illness and every obstacle to achieve what he wanted. Hopefully, Cleopatra took notice of him now, because this was the youth who would become Caesar's heir, and her enemy. While he waited outside Rome, ready to enter the city in triumph after the Spanish campaign against the last remnants of the Pompeians, Caesar wrote his will at his villa at Labici. In it he named Octavius as the heir to most of his fortune, and more important, in a codicil he adopted him as his son. For Cleopatra and Caesarion there was nothing, but it is quite likely that they had discussed this problem in advance. Whether Cleopatra knew of the contents of Caesar's will before it was made public is not elucidated, nor is it known whether Octavius knew of Caesar's intentions. In September 45, perhaps the only facts that the protagonists would know for certain were that Caesar looked upon both Cleopatra and his great-nephew favourably.

Caesar had not eradicated his enemies completely, since Pompey's younger son Sextus was still at large, chased from most provinces of the growing Empire but equipped with a fleet that he would use to harass Rome for several years to come. But for all intents and purposes the civil war was now over. Caesar could at last turn to the needs of Rome herself. He had enjoyed immense and unprecedented powers while he fought the various campaigns of the civil war. However, now that it was supposed to be at an end, there was no real reason why he should continue to enjoy them, except that he needed them in order to put his grand schemes into practice. Most of them were necessary and beneficial, and all of them sensible, but pushed through contrary to Roman custom, because Caesar was in a hurry and impatient of senatorial debate.

There is no recorded opposition to his reform of the calendar, whereby he established the means of reckoning time still current today. On the face of it, this is a straightforward enough procedure, but would require considerable influence to execute. Perhaps because everyone could see the necessity for it, the proposal did not meet with opposition. For a long time, due to the wars and upheavals, the ancient lunar calendar had not been adjusted as it should have been by the intercalation of extra days to ensure that the seasons matched the months to which they belonged. By the mid 40s BC the agricultural festivals were nowhere near the times when they were normally celebrated, and to bring them in line again before he established the solar calendar of 365 and a quarter days, Caesar inserted an extra three months into the year 46.

The calculations upon which the solar calendar were based were derived from Egyptian scholars, and the accredited source for Caesar's reform is Sosigenes, one of Cleopatra's entourage, so it is ultimately to her that the modern world owes its calendar. Her influence here does not need illumination, but there is disagreement about how much more she may have influenced Caesar in other areas of Roman politics and indeed how much she influenced him personally, either directly or indirectly. Certainly he had seen what Egyptian engineers were capable of, but his plans to drain the malaria-infested marshes around Rome may have been formed long ago before he had set foot in Egypt. He could see so sharply and clearly all that needed to be done to create in and around Rome a magnificent city, with all modern amenities, properly functioning and administered, but he was already advanced in years and felt that he had little time to spare. He could not and would not creep slowly forward by degrees, allowing the Senate to reject some of his ideas, while he carried through other schemes to completion. In his impatience he accrued powers to enable him to do what he wanted, hoping rather than imagining that a demonstration of leniency towards his opponents would mollify them sufficiently to permit him to do what he wanted unhindered, all for the ultimate benefit of Rome and the Romans. His famous *clementia*, his merciful and non-vindictive attitude only made people more nervous and irritated; they did not believe him, or they resented his presumption and what they saw as arrogance in elevating himself so far above them as to dispense mercy.

Autocracy seemed to be what he was aiming for, and people said that he had drawn his ideas in that sphere from Cleopatra, who probably coached him nightly in absolutism and ambition. Caesar only made matters worse by honouring her publicly. In his new Forum behind the Senate House, he built a temple to his divine ancestress Venus Genetrix, and placed inside it, as well as the statue of the goddess, a statue of Cleopatra. He had elevated her beyond anything that Roman men or women could even dream of, let alone realise. There would be much speculation about what he meant by this unusual action, and in a very short time the speculation would move on to what he was going to do next. Was Cleopatra to be made his consort, and set up as ruler of Rome as well as Egypt? Perhaps she was going to be declared a goddess, and everyone would have to worship her. Despite the universal hatred of her, the statue was not destroyed and survived for future generations of Romans to admire.

Cleopatra was blamed for all the ills that befell Rome since Caesar's victory over the Pompeians precisely because her arrival in Rome coincided with the frenetic schemes and gigantic reforms that Caesar proposed. She was distrusted because she was a foreigner, and what was even worse, a woman. Xenophobia and misogyny were not absent from the minds of ancient Romans. They reasoned that things had been bad enough before Caesar went to Egypt, but now that he had been there and succumbed to the baleful influence of the Queen, he was consumed by megalomaniac dreams of sole rule. So it seemed to those who could not trace the elements of Caesar's turbulent career back to its origins, or who had forgotten that Pompey had once been made sole consul, that he had governed his provinces via legates, and maintained or endeavoured to maintain a preponderant influence over those provinces that he did not govern. It was a sign of the times, a gradual evolution from magistrate, provincial governor and army commander in the employ of the state to independent warlord and potentate. There could have been worse masters than Caesar, and if he had not climbed his way to supremacy then sooner or later someone else would have taken his place.

Caesar did not flaunt power for the sake of it, but he used it to achieve what he considered best for Rome. The problem was that the Romans liked to be asked what was best for Rome and not to have it thrust upon them. Administrative reforms, drainage of the marshes, the creation of new Patrician families, the increase in the number of senators and magistrates, and the foundation of new colonies for veterans, were all sound procedures, and no doubt met with success, but people still distrusted a man who wielded that much power. Caesar tempered it very slightly. He did not hold the consulship each and every year, but everyone was aware that his election was a mere formality if he desired it, and he had been made Dictator several times, in 49, 48 and 46, imbued with powers that transcended those of the consuls. The office was usually adopted only in times of direst emergency and then for a limited duration, but it was becoming quite certain that he would use the powers conferred upon him to mould the Roman state into the pattern he decreed for it. He tried to reject the notion of kingship, which was anathema to the Romans, but it was an empty gesture. When his fellow consul Mark Antony offered him a diadem at the festival of the Lupercalia in February 44 he refused it theatrically, perhaps hoping to put an end to speculation as to his real intentions. It only made matters worse, because of the multiple interpretations of his motives: was he taken by surprise, did Antony try to do him a favour by enabling him to demonstrate that he did not want to be made king, or had they colluded to test the waters, in the hope that the populace would acclaim him king once given the opportunity? The situation was not helped by the fact that Caesar planned a fresh Parthian campaign to avenge the death and defeat of Crassus, and a passage in the Sybilline Books prophesied that Parthia could be conquered only by a king.

By this time the conspiracy to murder Caesar will have been formed, but perhaps not fully worked out in all its details. Brutus and Cassius are the two best known of this group, but there were over fifty men who were party to the plot, and behind them there were no doubt more who knew what was to happen and condoned it without being closely involved. Two factors precipitated the crisis. In February Caesar accepted the Dictatorship in perpetuity (*Dictator perpetuo*). This meant that it would be very difficult to remove him by any of the Republican procedures open to the senators who opposed him. Secondly he intended to leave Rome in March to attend to military problems on the Danube, and then to begin the Parthian campaign. To this end he had sent his great nephew Gaius Octavius, who had been made his master of horse (*magister equitum*), to Apollonia for the purpose of furthering his education, but in reality to gain experience of military life in Macedonia, where Caesar's legions were based in readiness for war on the Danube. The conspirators therefore decided that they had to act quickly before Caesar left. It had been bitterly obvious to them that even while he was hundreds of miles away, Caesar still dominated

Roman politics. If they had planned their assassination properly they would have massacred all Caesar's adherents as well, because his networks of associates were intricately woven and very deep, so it proved insufficient to attempt to unravel the whole fabric of Caesarian politics simply by removing the leader.

On 15 March the conspirators struck at the meeting of the Senate held in the assembly hall of Pompey's theatre, distracting Antony to detach him from Caesar's side as he entered the building. After the murder everyone fled. Antony shut himself up in his house expecting the worst, but when nothing happened he started to act very rapidly, summoning the Senate for a meeting two days later on 17 March in the temple of Tellus, close to his home and also not far removed from his soldiers. Miraculously he prevented a complete breakdown of law and order, and did not pursue the conspirators to avenge Caesar. Civil war was very near, but successfully averted. Cleopatra may have communicated with Antony about the situation. For a while everyone would lie low, tensely awaiting the outcome, and for a terrible moment both she and Antony probably imagined that assassins would be on their way to despatch them. It was probably difficult to believe at first that the conspirators had planned nothing beyond the murder of Caesar. They did not immediately take over the government and install themselves at its head, because their noble intentions were to rid themselves of arbitrary power, so to assume such power would be contrary to their ideals. They did not seem to have anticipated that a tremendous vacuum would be created after Caesar's death, and had not thought how to fill it. They proclaimed freedom, but since they had abolished all direction, anarchy was perilously close. Antony received little credit for picking up all the pieces and welding them back together.

Quite soon after Caesar's death, Cleopatra left Rome. She now had little reason to stay, uncertain perhaps of who were her friends and who were unsympathetic towards her. Caesar's death would precipitate several realignments which she did not have time to observe and analyse. She may have seen Antony before she departed, in order to ensure that her treaty arrangements were upheld and the claims of her son Caesarion were recognised. The contents of Caesar's will may not have surprised her in that there was no mention of either her or Caesarion, but Caesar could not have introduced political aims into what was supposedly a personal will. It may have come as a surprise

12 *Head of Mark Antony, as he may have appeared at the time of Caesar's*
assassination and the battle of Philippi. He was about 42 years old, the senior
statesman and general of his day, in command of most of the east after the defeat of
Brutus and Cassius. In 41 he summoned Cleopatra to Tarsus, where she arrived
in her famous Royal barge described by Plutarch.
Courtesy Capitoline Museum, Rome

that he named Gaius Octavius as his chief heir, though for those with sharp eyes and ears, the clues had already been revealed. There were no other relatives to whom Caesar could leave his fortune, and he obviously thought that his great nephew was deserving of such favours. He had promoted him along with other promising young men, but it was Octavius who had been sent on ahead to Apollonia and made master of horse. If Caesar had so wished he could have made alternative arrangements, ignoring Gaius Octavius altogether, but significantly he chose not to do so. Nor did he distribute his fortune equally among his friends. He did not even name Antony among the first echelons of his beneficiaries.

For the time being, the eighteen-year-old Gaius Octavius, soon to begin calling himself Gaius Julius Caesar, was not preponderantly significant. He was still in Apollonia with Caesar's legions, and so far he had not mobilised them for a march on Rome. He was so young, and continually ill, that most people probably discounted him as a contender in the political arena. The most pressing problem was who would succeed to Caesar's power and influence, and it now seemed that it would be Antony. Most of the anti-Caesarians dreaded his influence, but had been pleasantly surprised at his moderate behaviour. So far Antony had succeeded very well, and no-one could seriously fault him, except in so far as he had suddenly and suspiciously obtained money from somewhere to pay off all his huge debts, and he had taken charge of all Caesar's papers along with the Dictator's personal secretary, Faberius. Using these as his basis for action, he managed to persuade the Senate to ratify not only all the schemes that Caesar had begun, but also those he had merely planned and not yet brought to light. Not surprisingly, Antony was accused of all kinds of dishonest intentions, but since he had control of troops, and by now would have cultivated as many of Caesar's clients and supporters as he could, he was in a very strong position and the only man capable of solving the problems created by the removal of Caesar. Many men owed their offices and magistracies to Caesar, so to abolish all his acts as was first suggested involved the virtual dismantling of the government. On the other hand, to punish the conspirators would bring about an ongoing vendetta and destroy all that Caesar had achieved and tried to foster within the state. So there was a fragile truce, with the conspirators at first taking refuge on the Capitol Hill, until Antony coaxed them into coming to terms.

In these circumstances, with the Roman world reasonably quiet and Mark Antony striving to keep the peace, and Caesar's great nephew Gaius Octavius poised to enter history as he claimed his inheritance, Cleopatra sailed back to Egypt with Ptolemy XIV and the infant Caesarion.

3. Egypt and Rome

Precisely when Cleopatra returned to Egypt is not known. She probably stayed in Rome long enough to discover who would emerge at the head of the state, and whether there would be any advantage or dangers to herself and Egypt. She no doubt witnessed Caesar's funeral on 20 March, and appreciated Antony's outpouring of respect for Caesar in his famous speech, immortalised by Shakespeare, who portrayed Antony's mood accurately even if he did not reproduce the actual words. From Cicero's letters it can be deduced that by mid April 44 Cleopatra had left Italy, or that she was planning to leave quite soon. Cicero, studiously remaining away from Rome, wrote to Atticus on 15 April that he saw nothing to object to in her flight, implying that she had already gone. He used the word *fuga* to describe her departure, as though she had taken fright and fled. It was probably not so undignified as that, but Cicero could not interpret any of her actions in a good light, indeed he could scarcely bear to mention her by name, calling her the Queen in the letters where he referred to her.

The references to Cleopatra in Cicero's letters are tantalisingly unexplained, concerned with rumours about the Queen, some of which he said were diminishing by mid May, only to flare up again, perhaps about some other scandal, at the end of the month. Whatever it was, Cicero hoped that the story was true, so presumably it was not something beneficial to Cleopatra's interests or well-being. Some authors have used these references to Cleopatra to infer that she remained in Rome until the end of May or even later. Whether she was still in the city or not, there may have been some contact between her and Cicero in the early summer of 44, since after a silence about her lasting several days from the end of May, he launched into a tirade against her in mid June, writing to Atticus that he detested the Queen and her creatures. He complained that they treated him as though he had no feelings or spirit. In other words he had been insulted, but with Cicero it seemed that it was never very difficult to do that.

Consequently he declared that he would have nothing more to do with 'that lot' (*nihil igitur cum istis*). Perhaps Cleopatra had made overtures to him as a senator of considerable standing, whose eloquence could carry the day in a senatorial debate; she may have desired to win him over so as to have an effective mouthpiece in Rome. Caesar had not tried to silence Cicero, and in his turn Cicero was ambivalent and indecisive about Caesar, blowing hot and cold, wanting to like him but deciding that politically he could not allow himself to do so; but for all their mutual respect, it is obvious that they could never have worked together. Perhaps Cleopatra tried to recruit him in an attempt to keep him under control, rather than let him drift into the opposite camp; perhaps she hoped to reconcile him to Antony; or perhaps Cicero had been mortally affronted by what he considered a lack of due respect while Cleopatra was in Rome, and simply could not let the matter drop.

Cleopatra was probably back in Egypt by the late summer of 44. Her movements are not recorded in detail, but it is likely that she had already spent some time and effort in planning how to consolidate her position. Her chief Roman ally had disappeared, and so far no-one else of the same calibre had taken his place. She needed to create a strong government and sound economy before she had to face whichever of the Roman generals developed an interest in Egypt. She did not delude herself that Egypt and Rome could exist happily side by side, each going about their separate business. Thinking of the longer term, in order to establish herself and Caesarion as rulers of Egypt, she may have schemed to remove her brother. So far she had almost ignored the fifteen-year-old Ptolemy XIV, and had managed to keep him out of the clutches of any influential counsellors who might try to follow the example set by Pothinus and Achillas. As a boy Ptolemy XIV was perhaps amenable to her direction, but she may have feared that he would grow troublesome as he matured, striving for a greater share in her government and for more independence. Cleopatra could not spare the time for contradictory debate and certainly had no intention of allowing outright opposition to evolve. By September 44 Ptolemy XIV was dead, and Cleopatra shared her throne with her three-year-old son Caesarion, named Ptolemy XV Caesar, a deliberate declaration of an Egyptian and a Roman heritage.

The cause of death of Ptolemy XIV is not illuminated in any reliable source, allowing much speculation about it ranging from sudden illness to poisoning. The first century Jewish writer, Flavius Josephus, in no doubt that Cleopatra arranged her brother's death, opts for the latter method, but death by poisoning was a common and widespread accusation, often meaningless in an age which observed sensible religious precautions with regard to food, but was at the mercy of a hot climate without the benefit of refrigerators or rigorously enforced government control of food hygiene. However many excuses can be advanced in Cleopatra's defence, the removal of Ptolemy XIV was so fortuitous for her that it is quite natural that she should be accused by contemporaries and later authors of having him killed. No public outcry was recorded, which is not the same thing as saying that none ever occurred, but Ptolemy was perhaps successfully insulated from outside influence, with the result that only a few people knew him. If his household staff and his entourage were not inconvenienced by the death of their master, and were quietly absorbed into the Palace with their livelihoods intact, they no doubt had enough common sense to remain silent.

Secure as possible in her regime, with the undoubted opposition almost muzzled, Cleopatra could attend to the strengthening of Egypt, with eyes and ears constantly alert for what was happening in Rome. The fact that she was able to spend so much time away from Egypt without precipitating rebellions or riots attests to the fact that her ministers, officials and administrators operated efficiently, possibly even ruthlessly. She will have built up a following of loyal adherents, whose names are not known to us. Details of her administration are sketchy, and have to be extrapolated from general knowledge about Egypt under its Macedonian rulers. Perennial concerns were the food supply, religious observance, and for Alexandria, the control of trade. The Nile was not always dependable and was watched anxiously each year for signs of the likely flood levels and the consequent irrigation. There was an optimum level, within certain parameters; too much water was problematic; too little was disastrous. In the year of Pharsalus the inundations had been very disappointing; combined with the arrival of Pompey and then Caesar it seemed that the omens were bad. Religious observances were therefore very important in this respect, and Cleopatra ensured that all her subjects witnessed that she was scrupulous in attending to all aspects of ceremonial and sacrifice. She could not command the Nile to rise to optimum levels, but when all was well she could be seen to be effective, and when there were

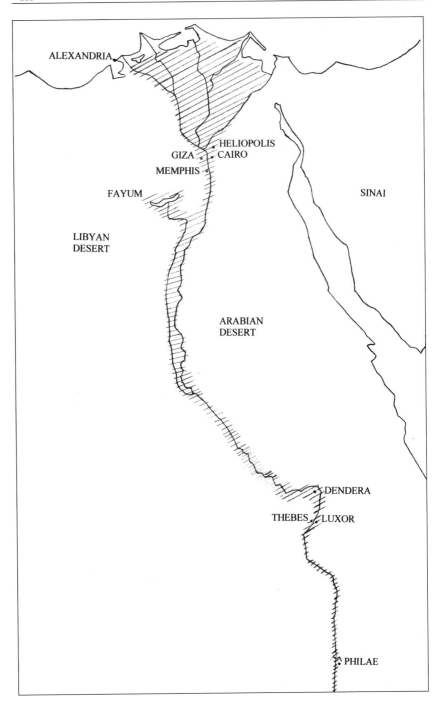

13 Map of Egypt showing the flood plain of the Nile, the source of Egypt's legendary wealth. Drawn by J.T. Taylor

problems, explanations could be found, the gods could be propitiated, and hopes could be focused on the following year.

Central control of food production had always been the responsibility of the rulers of Egypt. The Ptolemies as Pharaohs owned all the land and administered much of it directly; a vast bureaucracy monitored all aspects of leases to tenants, planting, harvesting, and taxation. Warehouses were under Ptolemaic control, so that when famine threatened, the rationing of food was so much simpler. Egypt was more or less self-sufficient in food production, but imports, especially of timber in a virtually treeless land were also necessary. No useful commodity was ignored, especially since all imports could be taxed. There were different rates for different items, all of it under Royal control. Cleopatra fostered trade and business deals outside Egypt, always aware of advantageous opportunities, as for instance when Antony supported Herod in his struggle for the throne of Judaea. When Herod finally became king with Antony's help, Cleopatra magnanimously took over the production of his balsam groves of Jericho, and leased them back to him for 200 talents a year. Modern monetary equivalents mean very little in days of rapid inflation; suffice it to say that it was a lot of money. She also regained all or most of that part of the kingdom of Nabataea which had once been under Ptolemaic control, taking over the monopoly on the production of bitumen, and making Herod responsible for collecting the annual rent for the land from Malchus, king of Nabataea. She invested time, effort and money only where it would bring profit.

She profited from her attention to the coinage, lowering the precious metal content but insisting upon assessing the coins at their old values. To make certain that merchants accepted them for what she said they were worth, she had the denominations marked on the coins. It seems such a common-sense, practical procedure, but it had not been done before. Cleopatra possessed sufficient power to enforce her regulations, and could watch her coffers grow fuller every day.

Issuing coins in her own name without any sign of a Royal consort, Cleopatra broke with precedent, not even pretending to share her throne for the sake of hallowed custom. Her portraits on her coinage show her with prominent nose, sometimes with a pronounced hook. Her hair is usually drawn tightly back and held by a head-band or diadem, with a plait rather like a bun at the back of her neck. The same severe hair style is to be seen on various sculptures of her, and helps to

14 *Cleopatra as the goddess Isis from the temple at Dendera. Photo David Brearley*

identify other portraits of her, but the style was probably copied by other women eager to emulate her.

In religious terms Cleopatra was identified with Isis, wife of Osiris, and Caesarion was equated with their son Horus. This was a particularly fortuitous circumstance since Horus was the avenger of his father; Caesarion was named Philopator, lover of his father, so the parallel between Osiris-Horus and Caesar-Caesarion will have been crystal clear. When Caesarion was born, Cleopatra issued coins with a representation of herself suckling the infant, which was equated with the many representations of Isis suckling Horus, labelled the Black Madonna by the Christians. On the walls of the temple at Hermonthis, where some years earlier Cleopatra attended the inauguration ceremony of Buchis, the sacred bull, sculptures show Cleopatra and Caesarion once again in association with Isis and Horus. The birth of Caesarion and that of Horus are shown side by side. Egyptian gods and goddesses surround Cleopatra and her son, placing them among the panoply of deities and proclaiming their divine rulership.

Cleopatra's concern for religion also embraced the Greek population, for whom Osiris, Isis and Horus were the Egyptian counterparts of Dionysus, Aphrodite and Eros. Alexander the Great had identified himself with Dionysus, and Cleopatra's father Ptolemy Auletes had proclaimed himself to be the New Dionysus. When Antony took charge of the eastern provinces, he too identified himself with Dionysus, who was held in great esteem by the peoples of the east. His association with Cleopatra as Isis-Aphrodite elevated them both to a higher plane than the merely mortal. In the east, people were comfortable with the divinity of their kings and queens. In Rome, living individuals were solidly earthbound, but they could claim divine descent if their ancestors hailed from the distant and mythical past. Exceptional people could become divine, but only after death, and so far only Romulus had enjoyed that distinction. Caesar traced his descent back to the goddess Venus, and towards the end of his career he may have been proclaimed a god while he still lived, but there is room for doubt, in that it may have been not instant deification, but a declaration of intent to deify him after his death. The distinction hardly matters, since posthumous deification was such a signal honour. Octavian made strenuous efforts to put this into effect, and assiduously claimed divine descent as the son of the god Julius Caesar (*divi Juli filius*). He respected Roman sensibilities to this extent, but was not averse to being proclaimed a god in the eastern provinces and worshipped as such. It provided a counterweight to Antony's influence, despite the fact that Antony had been given control of the east.

As commander of all the forces in the east, Antony inevitably came into contact with Cleopatra. She would be prepared for such circumstances, having watched events after the death of Caesar. The whole of the Roman world had been split into factions once Caesar was dead, and civil war had rapidly resumed. The young Gaius Octavius returned to Rome determined to claim his Caesarian inheritance. Antony accommodated him up to a point, but since he had achieved an uneasy and fragile peace and come to terms with Brutus and Cassius and the rest of the conspirators, he did not welcome the volubly publicised determination of the new Caesar to avenge the death of the old one, thereby upsetting all the pacificatory arrangements that Antony had patiently persuaded the Senate to accept.

Gaius Octavius was the main financial beneficiary of Caesar, but that was not all. He was now, according to Caesar's will, adopted into the family of the Julii Caesares as Caesar's son. According to Roman usage, he was entitled to call himself Gaius Julius Caesar Octavianus, indicating that his original family name was Octavius. The new Caesar never used the name Octavianus, insisting on using the same name as his adoptive father, but he is known to the modern world as Octavian in his youth, until he was finally honoured by his new name Augustus, bestowed on him by a grateful Senate long after Cleopatra and Antony were dead.

Octavian embarked on a campaign to have his adoption recognised, because it was probably a very shaky foundation for his political inheritance if it was not formally ratified by law. Adoption was usual in Roman law, but only while the two parties still lived. Adoption by last will and testament may not have been legal. Some modern scholars have traced similar cases in an attempt to prove that it was legal, and yet other scholars have dismissed them all to prove that such methods of adoption had no foundation in law. The latter are probably right. Certainly Octavian tried very hard in 44 while Antony was consul to have his adoption ratified. He was thwarted this time, but took care to have the law passed as soon as he became consul himself and was in a stronger position.

Towards the end of Antony's consulship, relations between him and the Senate deteriorated, despite the fact that he had prevented even the smallest riot and had averted civil war. Brutus and Cassius had been assigned duties in the provinces to remove them from Rome, but rather than take up what they considered to be ignominious positions, they took flight to the eastern provinces, took them over by force, and began recruiting. At this point, Cleopatra would need to tread very carefully. She and the assassins of Caesar were hardly likely to extend friendly overtures to each other, but Egyptian wealth would be very attractive, and either Brutus or Cassius might decide that they needed help, willingly given or otherwise.

Rome began to seethe with unrest. It seemed that the anti-Caesarians were determined to have war, stirred up by the inflammatory speeches of Cicero, who returned to the political scene in September 44. As consul Antony had assumed command in Caesar's place without adopting tyrannical measures, but nonetheless he was cast in the role of enemy of the state, perhaps because the Senate feared what he might do, rather than what he had done. After his consulship, he was supposed to go to Macedonia as governor, but he changed all this, preferring the province of Gaul, since it was closer to Italy and would provide a vantage point from which he could monitor and if necessary control events in Rome. He would have to remove Decimus Brutus, one of the assassins of Caesar, but still the properly appointed governor of Gaul. To help him in this task he brought over Caesar's legions from Macedonia. The Senate acquiesced but reacted badly. The scene was set for another civil war. Cicero launched into the second finest hour of his career, delivering clever and virulent speeches against Antony, known as the *Philippics* in comparison to the speeches of the Greek orator Demosthenes against Philip of Macedon.

In the end Antony withdrew to Gaul, where he met an intransigent Decimus Brutus. Antony was a vigorous and determined commander and he soon had Decimus bottled up in Mutina (the modern Modena) in northern Italy, but almost as quickly there was a senatorial army marching against him, sent to the rescue of Decimus. Octavian played his part alongside Cicero, because although he had an army formed from the many soldiers who were fiercely loyal to Caesar and were willing to follow Caesar's son, he was not in authorised command of troops. He needed legitimate power in the political and military spheres, and being under age and unqualified, he needed influential allies to ensure that he was given power. Cicero was probably blinded by anyone who listened attentively to him and kept their own counsel. Octavian was adept at both, and somehow persuaded the Senate that if he was given a military command he would help the two consuls for 43, Hirtius and Pansa, in the struggle against Antony. Quite why the Senate imagined that the adoptive son of Julius Caesar would attempt to rescue one of the assassins of Julius Caesar has never been satisfactorily explained. Octavian must have been a very good actor.

Antony won the first round against Hirtius and Pansa, but was defeated at the second of the two battles collectively known as Forum Gallorum, so he wasted no time in retreating from northern Italy into Gaul in mid April 43. The Senate rejoiced, because even though one of the consuls had been killed and the other had died of wounds, it seemed that Antony was removed for ever. The smug expectation was that Decimus Brutus and his troops, accompanied by the consular armies now under the control of Octavian, would make short work of Antony. Two factors dashed these hopes. Firstly, Antony was always at his best in a crisis, and managed to get his armies over the Alps more or less intact. Secondly, Octavian dawdled, delayed and prevaricated and did not help Decimus, whose troops deserted to Antony or ran away, leaving Decimus in a desperate situation. He was killed, possibly on the orders of Antony, by a Gallic chieftain.

In the summer of 43 Octavian revealed his hand. The consulship was vacant. He asked for it politely, by sending a delegation of his soldiers to Rome. The Senate refused. Octavian was too young at nineteen years old, and the Senate imagined that they could circumvent him now, because it seemed as though he and his troops were no longer necessary in the war against Antony. Only when they heard that Octavian was marching on Rome accompanied by eight legions did the senators start to scurry to their own defence. Two legions were summoned from Africa, another of raw recruits was put together from the remnants of the consular army, and finally representatives were sent to Octavian's troops with lots of ready cash to bribe them and tear them away from their commander. The soldiers kept the money, and the senatorial legions joined them.

Octavian was elected consul in August 43, with his cousin Pedius as colleague. Almost his first act was to have his adoption legalised, and his next was to condemn all of Caesar's murderers. Those who had not already fled from Rome, did so now to swell the forces of Brutus and Cassius in the east. Next, Octavian communicated with Antony, who by this time had amalgamated his troops with those of the governors of Spain and the other Gallic provinces. An alliance between Caesar's heir and Caesar's lieutenant had always been the most comfortable alternative, but Octavian had no bargaining power at first and might have been overwhelmed if he had become one of Antony's satellites. As consul he was now on a level with Antony, even if he could not muster enough troops to match Antony's 22 legions.

The two men met at Bologna on an island in the river, bringing in their colleague Lepidus as part of their alliance. Lepidus was a high-born and wealthy aristocrat, and was a confirmed Caesarian. As governor of Gallia Narbonensis he had vacillated slightly about joining Antony as he approached from across the Alps, but after Antony had walked into his camp he capitulated and brought his army over. He was declared an enemy of the state by the Senate, as Antony was. His fate was sealed from then on, and he became the third member of the Triumvirate, as the notorious alliance is known. The terms Triumvirate and Triumvirs are modern inventions; in Latin, Antony, Octavian and Lepidus were titled *Tresviri rei publicae constituendae*, or three men with responsibility for restoring the government of the Republic. Their powers were limited to five years; it was a wise precaution to put some control on their thinly veiled dominance, since the Romans had bitter experience of permanent powers. Between them the Triumvirs shared out the Roman world and command of all the troops. Lepidus was given control of his old province of Gallia Narbonensis and all of Spain; Octavian received Sardinia, Sicily and Africa, and Antony as the senior partner was to remain as governor of Cisalpine and Transalpine Gaul. They now needed to collect money, without which they could not hope to maintain their vast armies, and also to eradicate all actual and potential opposition. Once arrived in Rome they set in motion a horrendous series of proscriptions, condoning the murder of their enemies and the seizure of their property. It was not just senators who were targeted, but also their circle of clients and supporters, the men who acted as financial and business agents for senators, who as a class were forbidden to engage in trade themselves. The ensuing widespread panic engendered acts of despicable cruelty in eliminating some people and also unselfish heroism in rescuing others. Many potential victims fled to join Brutus and Cassius, but many more did not escape, among them Cicero, who hesitated and was lost. His head and hands were nailed to the speaker's platform, the Rostra, in front of the Senate

15 Gold coin (aureus) of 42 showing the head of Brutus on the obverse, and military trophies on the reverse. Brutus raised troops in the east, preparing for the inevitable civil war with Antony and Octavian. © British Museum

House, from which vantage point he had delivered the speeches reviling Antony. Perhaps for this reason, it is Antony who receives all the blame for the orator's death, but all the Triumvirs had something to gain by Cicero's removal. When she heard of his death, Cleopatra probably merely thought that it was about time.

In the meantime, while the Triumvirs gained strength in the west, the conspirators had also gained strength in the east. The last Caesarian foothold had already been swept aside very early in the proceedings in July 43, when Cornelius Dolabella had tried to take control of Syria, where he was sent as governor. He made a good start by eliminating Trebonius, the anti-Caesarian governor of Asia, on his way to his province, but Cassius got to Syria ahead of him, so he had to fight to win it. Cleopatra sent four legions to help Dolabella, drawn from the remnants of the Gabinians and the troops left by Caesar in Egypt. The third-century historian Dio records that in recognition of her assistance and loyalty, the Triumvirs officially sanctioned the establishment of Caesarion as her co-ruler, which implies that up to this moment, there was no such recognition of her promotion of her son. It is fortunate that some recognition was afforded her, since her legions were placed in a severe quandary when Dolabella was besieged in Laodicea, where he eventually committed suicide. The commander of Cleopatra's four legions probably had no choice now except to try to return to Egypt, harassed all the way by Cassius' eight legions, or to join Cassius and stay alive. The soldiers probably reasoned that they were far from their bases, and it was useless to fight for a lost cause. Caesar was dead, a memory only; Cassius as their new commander was as safe a bet as could be risked, because he had extorted money from the eastern provinces and was therefore likely to be able to pay the troops. He now made demands on Cleopatra for supplies of food and money. She advanced reasonable excuses rather than refuse him outright. The Nile floods had not been sufficient to produce good harvests, so Cleopatra had to husband her resources carefully; this was perfectly true, and perhaps Cassius had agents working for him who would be able to verify the story.

Having rid themselves of opposition at home, and gathered stupendous quantities of money by fair means or foul, mostly foul, all three Triumvirs declared war on the conspirators, who by that time were in full control of the east. It meant that the Triumvirs had to carry the war there and fight it out. Lepidus remained in Italy while Octavian and Antony ferried troops across the Adriatic, just as Caesar had done before Pharsalus. Cleopatra sent a fleet to assist them, but strong winds damaged some of the ships and forced them back to Egypt. She sailed with the fleet herself, in the flagship, demonstrating her loyalty to Caesar's avengers, and also risking her life into the bargain. She regained Alexandria safely, and there awaited the outcome of the war. Antony and Octavian brought it to a conclusion at the battle of Philippi in October 42. When the fighting was over, refugees from among the entourage of Brutus and Cassius, who were dead, joined Sextus Pompey and his pirate fleet. Except for full control of the Mediterranean, therefore, the Triumvirs were in command of the rest of the Roman world and could carve up the provinces between them to their mutual advantage. The new settlement readjusted some of the arrangements that they had made at their first conference at Bologna. Lepidus was suspected of sounding out Sextus Pompey, and was therefore distrusted. Eventually he received Africa as his province, but he was beginning to count for less and less as Antony, who had done most of the work in winning the battles, and Octavian became the main contenders for power. Octavian took Spain, Sardinia, Sicily, and Corsica, Antony retained control of Gaul and in addition was assigned

16 Gold coin (aureus) of 42 showing the head of Mark Antony with his title Triumvir (IIIVIR). On the reverse the god Mars rests his foot on a shield, indicating that war was the aim of the Triumvirs, to avenge the death of Caesar. © British Museum

to the whole of the east. Italy was supposed to be common ground to both Octavian and Antony, but it was Octavian who was based there and who was able to work steadily on the western half of the Empire to foster loyalty to himself.

Cleopatra re-entered the scene when Antony summoned her to meet him at Tarsus in southern Cilicia (modern Turkey), ostensibly to answer the charge that she had aided the conspirators. Antony had wintered in Athens in 42–41 and had been preoccupied in sorting out the tangled situation in the eastern provinces, as well as attending to the non-Roman neighbouring territories. He went to Pergamum first and called a conference of all the eastern states, which accordingly sent representatives to him. Brutus and Cassius had impoverished if not ruined many of these states by their demands for money and supplies. Those states that had aided the conspirators willingly had to be distinguished from those which had been forced into submission, and both of these categories differed from the few that had been able to resist demands. Some had been devastated as a result. In the midst of ameliorating situations in states like these, and punishing those states who had acted against the interests of the Triumvirs, Antony sent a summons to Cleopatra.

If the accusation was in fact made against her that she had aided the conspirators, both accuser and accused knew that it was grossly unfair. She had done all that she could to help the Triumvirs, but her efforts had been unsuccessful. Her legions sent to help Dolabella had deserted to Cassius, and the fleet she sent to aid Octavian and Antony had foundered. The accusation was an excuse to get her to come to Tarsus because Antony wanted something; the fact that she went means that she had something to gain. Antony and Cleopatra had much to offer each other. There was some wrangling before she came. Letters were sent to her, which she no doubt answered charmingly without committing herself, then Quintus Dellius was sent in person. His reputation was probably worse than Antony's for improper behaviour and non-Roman activities. Cleopatra probably found him great fun. She said she would come to Tarsus.

Antony was currently the most important figure in Roman politics, and was also one of Caesar's immediate associates. That made it all the more palatable to go to meet him. If Brutus or Cassius had emerged victorious from the battle of Philippi, Cleopatra would have still required diplomatic contact with them and the Roman Senate to keep Egypt intact and as free of Roman control as she could make it, but in that instance she would most likely have sent high ranking envoys. She would have been forced to recognise the immense power of the conspirators if they had eliminated the Triumvirs, but in a situation where she had no choice except to preserve amicable relations for the sake of her country, a personal audience with Caesar's murderers would have left her with a bitter taste in her mouth. If it had been Octavian or even Lepidus who had been given control of the eastern provinces, she would have treated with them on the best terms that she could extract, but perhaps would not have engaged in a more personal relationship, remaining strictly on business terms with them. With Antony, because she knew him already, and because he had been loyal to Caesar, bargaining to secure the autonomy of Egypt would be a more palatable task. Her own security and future development depended upon the favour of Rome, or at least upon the absence of hostilities. Sailing to Tarsus, she obviously hoped for something far better than that.

She dressed for the occasion. She was the Queen of Egypt coming to meet the Roman Triumvir, but since she was also Aphrodite coming to meet Dionysus, or in Roman terms, Venus coming to meet Bacchus, she set out to impress the natives, and from all accounts she succeeded. She set out from Alexandria in her famous Royal barge, propelled by its purple sail, a wonder to behold for the ancient world, and perhaps for the modern world, too. During excavations at the Royal port of the Ptolemies at Alexandria, archaeologists have found the remains of a ship 30 metres long in the private harbour of the Palace. This ship was sunk, probably by deliberate ramming; at any rate it somehow acquired a large hole in the hull. On board were remains of rigging, fine pottery, glassware, and jewellery. Radio-carbon-dating techniques have shown that the timbers were used sometime between 90 BC and AD 130, but unfortunately cannot give a more precise date for the ship. It cannot be linked unequivocally with Cleopatra, but it does demonstrate what her ship may have been like. Even if it finally proves not to be the Royal barge where Antony was entertained by the Queen of Egypt, it is an exciting find, revealing many details of ship construction and the daily life of its passengers and crew.

The legendary, splendid Royal ship conveyed Cleopatra up the river Cnydus, according to Plutarch, in swathes of precious perfumes, with handmaidens on each side and boys costumed as Cupids wafting fans over her, as she reclined under a canopy of cloth of gold. The description could go on and on, mounting superlative upon superlative. Joseph Mankiewicz's film *Cleopatra* may have exaggerated much and made mistakes of detail, but for the sheer consummate showmanship and the dazzling effect, the depiction of the Royal barge sailing to Tarsus was not far wrong. Cleopatra was a legend in her own lifetime. Now she was about to meet the other half of her legend. She entertained Antony to dinner on board ship. Plutarch says that it was brilliantly lit with an extraordinary number of lights. It was certainly lavishly equipped, and probably completely overwhelming. Antony tried to match her hospitality on the following night, but failed miserably. Plutarch describes how Cleopatra quickly assessed his character, full of bluff soldier's humour, and accordingly she adapted her own behaviour to suit his. Antony liked such women, and he already knew Cleopatra when she stayed in Rome as Caesar's guest, but perhaps he had not yet met this facet of her personality. He was probably swept off his feet on the spot.

4. Antony

Antony was planning a campaign against Parthia, and needed money, supplies, and a guarantee of peace and quiet behind him before he entered foreign territory. Initially it was Caesar's project, but now it had become more urgent, since the Parthians were restive on the borders of Syria, and besides the perceived threat to Roman territorial interests, the defeat of Crassus in 53 was still not avenged. The campaign did not get off to an immediate start, because the various states on the borders of Rome and Parthia were not yet strengthened and bound as far as possible in allegiance to Rome. Antony worked hard to achieve this but nonetheless he has been accused of neglecting his duties in these respects, abandoning his governors and generals to deal with whatever arose, while he tamely followed Cleopatra to Egypt for the winter of 41–40. His apparent readiness to recognise and gradually confirm Cleopatra's claims to eastern territories that had once formed the Ptolemaic Empire sealed his fate for the future. The fact that he did not accede to all that Cleopatra allegedly demanded over the years never vindicated him.

As an essential priority in 41, Cleopatra cleared away all remaining opposition to her rule. Her half sister Arsinoe was at Ephesus, supposedly safe in the sanctuary of the great temple, but the High Priest was prepared to call her Queen, either because she insisted upon it, or because he wished to honour her without thinking of the effect it may have when Cleopatra heard of it. Arsinoe as Queen of exactly what and where was not clearly outlined, but that was not important. Arsinoe's ambitions had to be nipped in the bud in case she started a revolution or one was started in her name. Cleopatra could cope with her half sister as a martyr far better than she could cope with her alive and potentially dangerous. Presumably acting upon Cleopatra's express wishes, Antony gave orders for the execution of Arsinoe. The High Priest was spared, though it was said that Cleopatra wanted him

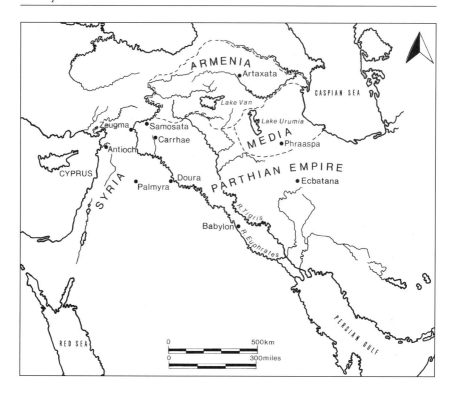

17 *Map to illustrate Antony's eastern campaigns. Before the war began, Ventidius Bassus drove the invading Parthians out of Syria and besieged the last die-hards at Samosata. Antony invaded in 36, assembling his army at Zeugma, to make it seem that he was about to launch an attack from that point into Parthia, perhaps to avenge the defeat of Crassus at Carrhae, which lay to the east of Zeugma. That was not his intention at all but perhaps served to distract the Parthians while he then made a dash northwards into Armenia to come down behind the Parthians after attacking Phraaspa. Unfortunately all his plans were thwarted there. He lost his siege train, Phraaspa did not fall to him, his allies began to desert and he had to retreat through Armenia. Drawn by Graeme Stobbs*

executed along with her sister. Antony intervened, so it was understood, curbing Cleopatra's blood lust.

The next to be removed was Serapion, the Ptolemaic governor of Cyprus, who had sided with or even supported Cassius when he arrived in the east before Philippi, and took control of Syria. Perhaps the presence of Roman troops so close to him made Serapion nervous. He could not be certain that the Triumvirs would arrive in the east to fight Cassius, and at that early stage in the wars it was not even a safe bet that they would win. Syria was much closer to Cyprus than Rome, so Serapion probably made what seemed the wisest decision at the time. As a naval base, Cyprus would be invaluable to the conspirators, so if he did not allow them in, they may have arrived in force, destroying as they went. The peaceful alternative probably seemed the better one. He most likely acted on his own initiative; he certainly would not have received instructions from Cleopatra to aid and abet the murderers of Caesar, but just in case there was any suspicion that she was duplicitous and had hedged her bets with regard to Cassius, Cleopatra positively had to have Serapion executed, not so much to prove his guilt as to prove her own innocence. Allegedly she had been summoned to Tarsus to answer the charge that she had not exactly been totally loyal to the Triumvirs and may even have helped the conspirators. The governor of Cyprus was the weak link in her defence, so he could not be pardoned and then pensioned off with a warning not to do it again. For Cleopatra, it was essential to show Antony that she had no hesitation in removing people disloyal to the Triumvirs. It was equally vital to demonstrate to the rest of her Egyptian and Alexandrian officials that her word was law, that disobedience or acting without orders would be punished. Antony would endorse the execution because he was engaged in rooting out the vestiges of any support for the murderers of Caesar, so he made his intentions towards them very clear. Both Antony and Cleopatra would have every reason, though different ones, for executing Serapion.

This was not the end of the executions. A pretender to the Egyptian throne had set himself up in the east, claiming to be the revived Ptolemy XIII, who had drowned in the Nile. The fact that Caesar had dragged the body out of the river and put it on display failed to deter the pretender or his adherents. Such a display reached only a tiny audience in the north of Egypt, perhaps even limited to Alexandria. It would be a simple matter to convince people of other eastern provinces

18 *Head of Cleopatra with her severe hairstyle which is also depicted on her coins, and was emulated by other women in Egypt, as sculptures and portraits attest.*
Courtesy Vatican Museums, Vatican City

that the body was someone else's, and that Caesar and Cleopatra had conspired to make it seem as though Ptolemy was dead. Communications were not instantaneous, and news was not capable of proof in the ancient world, which lacked anything like television and newspapers carrying photos to the remotest parts of the country. As a political stunt, it was feasible, and after all, Egypt was worth the risks incurred in attempting to gain it. Whoever this man was, he chose the wrong time to incur these risks, when Antony commanded most of the east and had troops all over it. The inevitable result was another execution. Cleopatra could keep a closer watch on her territorial acquisitions with her current enemies removed.

Perhaps it was at this time that Antony attended to the problems of Judaea. In his youth as a cavalry commander in the army of Gabinius he had his first battle experiences in Judaea, in an effort to settle the problem of who was to rule the country. As Triumvir, he supported Hyrcanus as ruler, with the capable brothers Phasael and Herod as his administrators. For a short time there would be stability in Judaea, until the Parthians intervened. The details of what other political arrangements Antony and Cleopatra achieved at Tarsus are lost, submerged under a welter of Augustan propaganda that sought to cast Antony as a lost cause from the moment that he set eyes on Cleopatra and was seduced by her in 41. Octavian was careful not to portray Antony as the enemy of Rome, but rather Cleopatra whose influence over him was absolute. Her increasing power and wealth, her control of large parts of the east, and the closeness of Egypt to Rome, placed her in a unique position. Other states at other times were more malleable, or were eventually conquered and then exploited for whatever reason the Romans chose to name. Egypt was different, and threatening. If Cleopatra and Antony chose to combine in the east, the power bloc so formed would overshadow anything the west had to offer Octavian. The civil war that ended with the battle of Actium in 31 and the fall of Alexandria to Octavian in 30, however far back its origins can be pushed, and however inevitable it may have been, began in earnest in 41 at Tarsus.

Antony's visit to Egypt at the end of 41 has become the stuff of romance and legend. He arrived there as a private citizen, not as Roman Triumvir or conquering general, nor even strictly as a Roman. Antony liked to dress as a Greek, and whenever he was in Athens, where he had gone to study as a young man, he adapted willingly to the

Greek way of life. He had been to Alexandria before and knew of the volubly expressed opinions of the inhabitants; he had nothing to gain by descending upon them in an official capacity. Cleopatra staged endless parties and celebrations, displaying the resources that Egypt could offer. Enjoyment was the order of the day while politics, never entirely forgotten, were relegated to the background. On a fishing trip, Antony cheated boisterously, despatching some of his slaves to attach some freshly-killed fish to his line so he could pretend that he had caught more than anyone else in one fell swoop. Cleopatra probably planned her response there and then, but waited. On the next fishing trip, she sent her slaves to hook up a salted fish to his line. Antony was delighted; childish fun emanating from a Roman Triumvir and a Queen of Egypt in no way diminishes their stature and brings them closer to the modern world as understandable human beings. There seems to have been no serious objection to their behaviour from the Egyptians or the Alexandrians. Cleopatra had enemies among the higher echelons of both communities, but fortunately the Alexandrians already knew Antony and his predilections, and for the most part they liked him; he was so refreshingly different from other stuffy Romans, most of them continually prattling about virtue and proper Roman gravitas, and all of them sure of Rome's supremacy to any other race or country. Antony was more tolerant, ready to adopt Greek fashions, or any other way of life that suited him; at ease with himself, Antony absorbed experience and all that life had to offer. He formed the Society of Inimitable Livers, or those who lived like nobody else. Though the pun does not work in Greek or Latin, Antony was not only an Inimitable Liver himself, but he must also have possessed an inimitable liver to cope with the Herculean banquets and the constant flow of wine which Cleopatra kept pouring in his direction.

Antony deserved a holiday. He had lived through an extremely hectic three or four years from his consulship in 44 to his visit to Alexandria. During that time he had seen his friend and mentor murdered in Rome, then been exiled and declared an enemy, crossed the Alps in early spring snows and nearly starved to death, fought his way back to power in an unforgivably but necessarily ruthless manner, planned and won the campaign of Philippi, and begun to sort out the tangled politics of the eastern states. If the Queen of Egypt had proved intractable, he would have eventually arranged an agreement with her, probably with difficulty, but since she was offering all that Egypt had to

19 Head of Mark Antony in his later years. It compares well with the heavy, square-jawed portraits on his coins, and with the head from the Capitoline Museum, Rome (10). Courtesy Musée Archéologique, Narbonne. Photo Jean Lepage © Musées de Narbonne

give him, including herself, he did not think twice about refusing. The Queen was unmarried and a free agent, and she had no consort except her son Caesarion who was not yet featured on coins or in any official capacity, so there was no risk of political scandal in Egypt in his association with the Queen. On a personal level, it did not seem that she had any jealous lovers hovering in the background ready to stab him on a dark night. Antony and Cleopatra have gone down in history as famous lovers, and the legend may be better and greater than reality. When Cleopatra gave birth to the twins Alexander and Cleopatra in the autumn of 40, some months after Antony had left Egypt, no-one was in any doubt as to the identity of their father, and Antony acknowledged them as his own.

Communications with Rome in the winter may not have been extensive. Sea voyages were not easy, and the overland route was long. Caesar sent no despatches to Rome for several months when he was in Alexandria, so perhaps Antony followed suit, but the accusations that he had forgotten Rome and his wife Fulvia are not entirely fair. Fulvia knew him well, and was aware of his reputation as an inveterate womaniser when she married him, so she cannot realistically have expected that he would suddenly turn into a monogamous and faithful husband. She probably loved Antony enough to allow him to do exactly as he liked, and in her turn she too was allowed far more licence than most Roman wives, to the disgust of sterner Roman men who disapproved of her. Fulvia was never a wife who stayed demurely at home looking after the house and family; she probably never even learned how to spin and weave and never touched a sewing needle in her life. Women were forbidden to enter politics, so they had no choice but to experience that life at second hand through their husbands. Antony knew all this when he married her, so neither of them had any illusions about each other. Unfortunately the sterile facts of history are that Antony had his famous affair with Cleopatra and cruelly abandoned his wife, but there may be subtler interpretations than that. Fulvia seems to have had his best interests permanently at heart, and it may be that the world has adopted an indignant stance on her behalf, when in fact she did not need sympathy.

While Antony and Cleopatra were living life to the full in Alexandria, Fulvia was instrumental in stirring up trouble for Octavian in Italy, acting in concert with Antony's younger brother Lucius Antonius, who was consul in 41. People described that year as the consulship of Lucius and Fulvia, which demonstrates how influential she was in political life. It was said by contemporaries that she merely wanted to create a rift between her husband and his fellow Triumvir so that Antony would have to return to Rome. Others both ancient and modern have speculated whether she acted on her own initiative, or whether Antony had sent her instructions. All the problems were centered around the discharged soldiers who were taken back to Italy after the battle of Philippi. First of all, Lucius accused Octavian of treating Antony's retired soldiers unfairly in the land settlements. Octavian countered by allowing Antony's own agents to oversee the settlements. When there was no more mileage to be gained on that question, Lucius found another cause to champion in the case of the farmers who were displaced to make room for the veteran soldiers. The eventual result of this manoeuvring was a minor but bloody civil war. The troops themselves tried to avert it by arranging a conference between Lucius and Octavian, but nothing came of it. Next, Lucius and Fulvia made it known that they were in danger from Octavian and decamped to Praeneste; Octavian recruited an army, put his friend Marcus Vipsanius Agrippa in command of it, and cut off Lucius from Rome, chasing him to Perusia (modern Perugia), where he put him under siege. At the beginning of 40, Lucius capitulated, and was exiled to Spain, his life spared but his freedom curtailed by Octavian's provincial governor and his ubiquitous agents. Fulvia sailed to Athens, and Antony's mother left Rome as well, to be rescued finally by Sextus Pompey, and ferried to Antony in Athens.

No-one knew then and no-one knows now whether Antony and Cleopatra were aware of what was happening in Rome. The affair is very strange, in that there was nothing solid to be gained from the troubles. If Antony had wanted to topple Octavian from power there were more useful ways of doing it; if he had briefed Lucius and Fulvia and then left them to achieve what he wanted by any means open to them, they bungled the job; if they acted on their own initiative, they did not do much better. The purpose may originally have been to create so much mayhem that the state would lapse into chaos, and then Antony could reappear in Rome as a saviour and restore order and calm. This was an old trick of Pompey's; he observed events without doing or saying very much, and waited to be asked to save the state, then burst into rapid, tremendously efficient and effective action, which presumably meant that he had already thought long and hard about how to retrieve the situation whichever way it went. Antony had seen Pompey at work at first hand, and may have taken a leaf out of his book. If he could demonstrate that Italy was at risk from the inept government of Octavian, then he could clear a path to power for himself, and eliminate Octavian because he would be discredited sufficiently to prevent him gaining the upper hand for some time. Lepidus was already fading into insignificance and in any case Antony had easily persuaded him to join him in the troubles of 43, so it would no doubt be possible to overawe him once again. The Triumvirate could then be abolished in favour of bestowing a less anomalous office upon Antony, and he would be in command of the west and the east. The theory is sound; the problem is still lack of certainty as to whose idea this may have been.

The crucial question concerns Antony's personal ambitions, and to what extent he perceived Octavian as a rival who must eventually be eliminated. He still had control of Gaul at this stage, and by dint of the armies there he had some control at a distance of what went on in Italy, which was supposed to be common ground for both Octavian and Antony. His tasks in the east were monumental, so it is questionable whether he really wanted to take on the west as well, except in so far as to retain his command in Gaul. But his fatal association with Cleopatra had begun, and Octavian used it to good effect, bringing it to fruition sometime later, when his portrayal of Antony made it seem as though he had betrayed Rome almost immediately after Philippi, engaging in all things shockingly un-Roman, bewitched by the evil Egyptian Queen. It may have been during the Perusine war that Octavian conceived the idea that Antony had fomented the troubles via his wife and his brother, that he was scheming to conquer the whole Roman world, and that Cleopatra was to blame for it. This is not to say that Octavian believed it, merely that he would know precisely how to use such inflammatory information, let out piecemeal, a suggestion here, a small hint there, a puzzled question as to Antony's motives, the sudden incredulous dawning that Cleopatra might possibly be aiming at world domination. Octavian's methods were subtle and infinitely patient, ever conscious of the longer term. When the time came to declare war on Cleopatra, and via her on Antony, Octavian succeeded in rousing all of Rome, Italy and the western provinces against them both in what seems like a very short time. In truth he probably sowed the seeds many years earlier, and then sat back to watch for and seize the perfect moment.

Apologists declare that Antony was innocent of any intrigue, a victim of the misguided attempts of Lucius and Fulvia to advance his cause and to remove Octavian. It is sometimes stated without qualification and without any evidence that he was shocked by developments in Italy. Such certainty is not possible, but Antony is exonerated by his consistent attitude towards Octavian after the Perusine war. When Octavian was engaged in the long struggle against Sextus Pompey and asked for help more than once in the form of political support, money, troops and ships, Antony gave it without hesitation, receiving very little in return, not even all that was promised him. His Parthian project was delayed three times because of Octavian's demands. Antony's actions after the troubles of 41–40 are not those of a power-crazed tyrant bent on world domination, nor are they those of a man who had attempted to subdue his rival, failed, and then lost his nerve. Most likely for this reason, that Antony was not the arch-enemy he painted him as, and for political correctness as well, Octavian was forced to concentrate all his enmity on Cleopatra in order to eliminate Antony. Even when civil war was very close, Octavian had to work extremely hard to rouse the Senate and the Roman people against Antony himself, because Antony countered most charges against him with reasonable equanimity. To cast Cleopatra as the real enemy was easier, because she was a foreigner, perhaps more alien than any of Rome's northern neighbours, and infinitely more to be feared because of her inexhaustible wealth and her acquisitive urges towards the eastern territories, usually those where there were commodities that Egypt required, access to the sea and vast potential for trade. It was easy to make much of her insatiable greed because it seemed that she did not know where to stop and would go on acquiring territories, whether they had anything to offer her or not, simply because she craved power. The fact that she was a woman, more closely involved with Antony than any other eastern monarch, played into Octavian's hands. If Cleopatra had been a man, Egypt would still have become the enemy of Rome because of the growing influence over large areas of the east, but it would have been much more difficult to accuse Antony of being mesmerised and consequently spineless.

Even if he did not know what was happening in Italy, Antony kept an eye on developments in the east while he was at Alexandria. He had left reliable generals in command of the eastern provinces, and had opened up negotiations, not yet completed, with the states bordering the Roman and Parthian territories. Antony's achievements in the east are commonly derided, despite the fact that there is no solid evidence apart from later Augustan propaganda that he failed in his task. Lack of verifiable detail goes against him because it seems as though he did nothing, going off to Alexandria in gross dereliction of duty. But the east demanded time and patience; results were not obtained by high-handed rapid coercion. That would have been disastrous. Each state and piece of territory demanded individual consideration, not only on its own account but also from the point of view of its neighbours. Arrangements made in one state caused ripple effects in others. The most important fact is that though he did not live to witness how far he was successful, Antony's eastern policies bore fruit later. After the battle of Actium when Octavian was left in supreme command of the Roman Empire, he did not have to set in motion a radical reorganisation of the east. The kings, princes and overlords who had been loyal to Antony came to the sensible conclusion that it was not worth losing their thrones by opposing the victorious Octavian just for the sake of it. Antony was dead, and to continue a war that was never theirs in the first place was futile. For the most part Octavian left them alone, making a few adjustments and adaptations according to circumstances, and monitoring events closely from then onwards. If it were true that Antony had created havoc in the east, Octavian's task after Actium would have been so much the harder, if not impossible.

The Parthian attack under Pacorus, the son of king Orodes, was encouraged by the Republican Quintus Labienus. He was the son of Titus Labienus, who was for many years Caesar's able lieutenant in Gaul, but then Pompey's man when civil war broke out. His son Quintus accompanied Brutus and Cassius to the east, and had been sent on a diplomatic mission to ask for help from the Parthians. He had become stranded there because Antony and Octavian won the battle of Philippi before he could return to the conspirators with Parthian aid. Now he instigated and encouraged attacks on Roman territory in the east. The situation was serious, demanding retaliation. In the spring of 40, Antony left Alexandria, and the pregnant Cleopatra, to attend to the problem. They were not to see each other again for nearly four years.

Antony's policy, still in its early stages, was clearly to strengthen the east and slowly foster stability in as many states as possible by installing and supporting pro-Roman rulers. Alarmed, the Parthians mounted a pre-emptive strike into Syria and Judaea, where they forced the Romans out, unseated the pro-Roman rulers and installed pro-Parthian candidates in their place. In Judaea they installed Antigonus. Antony's ruler Hyrcanus was deported, and of the two brothers whom Antony had appointed administrators, Phasael was killed, and Herod managed to escape with great difficulty. He arrived on the borders of Egypt and was given sanctuary by Cleopatra. When he was ready she furnished him with the means to go to Rome. Their relationship was amicable, especially in the face of a common enemy. Neither of them had anything to hope for from the Parthians, and both of them rested all their hopes on Antony. Some years later they would clash over territorial concerns, as Cleopatra reclaimed the coastal ports of the old Ptolemaic Empire, but for the moment Cleopatra had no reason to refuse to help Herod, because the prospect of a Parthian controlled Judaea was extremely uncomfortable, and Herod had every reason to be grateful.

Antony did not deal with the Parthian problem in person, because his relationship with Octavian had been seriously jeopardised by the agitations of Lucius and Fulvia. It was essential to repair this breach before it worsened, wrecking the peace that had been achieved after Philippi, and even worse, compromising Antony in the struggle against Parthia. He went to Greece and met Fulvia, berating her, it is said, for the trouble she had caused him. There is no reliable source for this. It is an assumption that happens to fit the theory that Antony had not been aware of what was happening in Italy, and it derives from the fact that he left Fulvia behind when he sailed to met Octavian. Antony could not afford to wait, and Fulvia could not have made the journey with him because she was very ill. She died shortly after his departure. The terms on which they separated are not known. His affair with Cleopatra and her troublesome behaviour in Italy lend themselves to the suggestion that it cannot have been an amicable parting, but modern ideals may not have applied in this instance. State business overruled personal emotions, and Fulvia would have approved of Antony's leaving her, even if she regretted it.

Antony's mother Julia had been given sanctuary by Sextus Pompey, who at some point put forward tentative suggestions for an alliance between himself and Antony, presumably for the purpose of neutralising or eventually eliminating Octavian. Sextus would have been a powerful assistant because he commanded a large and effective fleet, but he was not politically sound. He had cut off Rome's food supply and could do it again whenever he chose. Antony decided it was not the right time to form an alliance of this sort, because he aimed at reconciliation with Octavian. Instead he allied with the Republican Domitius Ahenobarbus, whose fleet had been roaming the Mediterranean ever since Pompey's defeat at Pharsalus. However, unlike Sextus, Domitius had not ventured to interfere with the shipping that carried the food supply of Rome.

There was a need for haste in reaching Italy, because at some time during the summer, Antony's legate Calenus, in command of the legions in Gaul, had died. Octavian had blithely taken over the troops. He protested that he did so in order to prevent a mutiny or the emergence of any other commander who might take control. There was always the lurking fear that any commander in Gaul might try to emulate Caesar and descend on Italy, so the Senate would endorse what Octavian had done. Significantly, Antony never regained his command of Gaul, so from that moment, no matter how many agreements he entered into with Octavian, his influence in the west was weakened.

When Antony and Domitius Ahenobarbus approached Italy, they discovered that the main port of Brundisium was closed to them, and the whole area was bristling with Octavian's troops. It looked very much as though Octavian had arranged all this deliberately, so Antony besieged the town, and took Sipontum nearby. The fighting that resulted was stopped largely by the soldiers themselves, who did not look favourably upon having to kill each other when they had once fought together for Caesar. In September 40 Octavian and Antony began to talk to each other. The outcome was the treaty of Brundisium, which redefined the Roman world into eastern and western portions, commanded by Antony and Octavian respectively. Lepidus was left in charge of Africa, where much of the corn that fed Rome was grown; it was an important command, but did not impinge too much on the responsibilities of the other Triumvirs, and had the advantage of removing Lepidus from Rome so that he would have to work hard to strike out on his own account. Octavian's task was to wrest control of the Mediterranean from Sextus, and Antony's was to force the Parthians out of the eastern provinces and carry the war into Parthia itself.

Antony and Octavian travelled to Rome, to celebrate their agreement and proclaim peace to the Romans, peace between themselves, that is;

20 *Silver coin with the heads of Antony and his new wife Octavia. Antony is described as IMP. COS. DESIG. ITER. ET TERT, indicating that he was designated for his third consulship for 38. The god Bacchus, or his Greek equivalent Dionysus is shown on the reverse, with two flanking serpents. Antony identified himself with Dionysus, the most renowned and powerful god of the east, with a pronounced appetite for wine. © British Museum*

the fact that wars were waged in other parts of the Roman world never seemed to bother the inhabitants of the capital city. The mutual connections between Octavian and Antony, deriving originally from Julius Caesar, were underlined now, when Antony was made a priest of the cult of the divine Caesar. To Cleopatra, who thoroughly understood and knew how to use the assets of divine monarchy, this would seem the logical conclusion of Caesar's power. It would also emphasise her association with Caesar and translate him into terms which the Egyptian population could grasp with ease. The cult of divine Caesar spread over the Roman world, fostered by Octavian for his own ends, but it also meant that the position of Caesarion as descendant of a Ptolemaic Queen and a divine Roman ruler would be considerably strengthened, particularly in the east, where Cleopatra's interests lay.

To seal the bargains made at Brundisium, a marriage was arranged between Octavian's sister Octavia, and Antony. Special dispensation was sought and received from the Senate to allow Octavia to marry, since her first husband Marcellus had only recently died and she had not yet completed the obligatory ten months of mourning. Wifely respect for the dead husband was not the most significant aspect of this ten-month interlude between marriages. It was a necessary measure so that the paternity of children born posthumously could be established with some degree of certainty. In Octavia's case, the normal rules were waived, and the children eventually born to Antony were undoubtedly his.

It would be a short while before Cleopatra heard of this marriage. Her reaction is not recorded, only surmised. The news may have arrived just after she had given birth to Antony's twins, a boy and a girl, whom she named Alexander and Cleopatra. In many ways, history was repeating itself in that she gave birth to Caesarion after Caesar left her, and now she bore two children to Antony without knowing whether he would return to her. The important elements in each case were that she had definite and securely attested affiliations, in more ways than one, with the leading Romans of the day, continuing the associations with Rome that her father and previous Ptolemies had established. That may have been the essence of what she wanted, to ensure that as far as possible there was a friendly faction in Rome, the strongest that she could associate with, which would shield her and Egypt from the predatory inclinations of other factions. Undying love ranked well below this vital consideration. She probably loved Antony very deeply, but could never realistically hope to force him to love her, nor to keep him permanently at her side. It is Roman propaganda that invents that wish for her, a concept that has been thoroughly absorbed by tradition ever since. In reality, a tamed Antony tied to her apron strings in Alexandria was of no use to her. She required a mostly compliant Antony, strong and active in the wider world, achieving significant results, remaining in power, representing Rome and on occasion bringing benefits to Egypt. The fact that he was now married to Octavian's sister did not mean that he had changed allegiance or had deserted her. There was great potential in the alliance in that it redefined responsibilities and gave Antony a stronger and reaffirmed hold on the east.

Taking advantage of his stay in Rome, Antony managed to persuade the Senate to ratify all his arrangements in the eastern territories, and to endorse in advance all that he had yet to do. He probably outlined in his speech what was still to be achieved, without giving away too much constricting detail. His powers as Triumvir were not in doubt, but there was a five year limit on them, due to expire in two year's time in

38. Though he and Octavian must have thought about what to do when their powers legally came to an end, individually if not in tandem, they made no mention of any plans to extend the term at this point. They adopted a tacit policy of least said, soonest mended, and no-one seems to have raised the issue with them.

The celebrations after the treaty of Brundisium were marred by the response of Sextus Pompey. He had not received any recognition from the terms of the treaty, so he used his usual weapon of attacking ports and disrupting the food supply. The population of Rome made it clear by rioting that they thought it was the responsibility the Triumvirs to do something about it. Octavian tried to make a speech, but the mob showered him with stones. Antony sent his troops to rescue him. The two of them had no choice now except to act in concert and to be seen to be trying to solve the problem of Sextus. The plain truth was that the Triumvirs were not yet in any position to stop Sextus' raids. Their fleet was negligible compared to his and their sailors were nowhere near as experienced. Antony had not yet begun his campaign in the east, and the Parthians were still in control or large parts of what was either Roman territory or that of Roman allies. With regard to Sextus, the only solution for the time being, and probably all the participants knew it was for the time being, was to arrange comfortable terms by diplomatic arrangement. In the summer of 39, the two Triumvirs met Sextus at Misenum, where they formally entered into a treaty named after the town. Sextus was magnanimously allowed to keep the islands which the Triumvirs were not strong enough to take from him, and he was integrated into the Roman world once more, being promised the consulship for 33, and control of the Peloponnese which Antony was supposed to cede to him. He was not given anything immediately, perhaps to allow him to prove that he could refrain from disrupting the food supply for some time, and to allow the Triumvirs some breathing space.

After the talks, there was a banquet on board Sextus' flagship. To demonstrate their trust, Antony and Octavian attended the festivities, perhaps with ships standing innocently by, watching for movement. Sextus' admiral Menodorus pointed out how easy it would be to set sail with the two eminent guests, and despatch them once and for all. Perhaps Sextus thought about it for a moment, drooling. The fact that he decided against it may merely have derived from the realisation that while he had command of the sea, he had not enough influence with the Senate, the population of Rome, or the vast armies of the Triumvirs to step into their shoes. It would seal his fate as a perpetual homeless pirate; the treaty of Misenum at least offered him a route into Roman politics, one which had been denied to him because his father's defeat came before he had begun an ordinary career.

During the winter of 39, Antony was at Athens with his new wife. He may have corresponded with Cleopatra, and may have known already of the birth of his two children the previous year. It is a question that no-one can answer, whether letters were shipped across the Mediterranean, of a personal or official nature. The campaign to restore the balance of power in the east had begun in the summer, under Antony's general Ventidius Bassus. This man was a capable officer who had started his career at the bottom of the ladder, and risen from the ranks. After Antony was defeated at the battle of Forum Gallorum in 44 and retreated across the Alps, Ventidius raised three legions for him in Italy and led them himself through territory watched by senatorial troops, to join up with Antony in Gaul. He had been useful after the Perusine war, too, when he collected Antonian troops and kept them out of harm's way while Octavian wreaked revenge on Lucius' men and on Perusia itself.

Antony chose the best general for the task of evicting the Parthians. Ventidius chased Labienus into oblivion, then drove the Parthians out of Syria. Peace was restored for the winter of 39–38, and Ventidius levied taxes on the cities that had helped Labienus and the Parthian king Pacorus. Antony left Athens in the spring of 38 to attend to the multiple problems of the eastern states, but was once more called to Italy to render assistance to Octavian. The treaty with Sextus had broken down quite soon, but Octavian had been badly defeated at sea. His standing in Rome was now very shaky, and he needed ships from Antony to replace his losses. Dutifully, Antony went to Brundisium, but Octavian failed to appear. Raging at the loss of time, Antony hurried to Syria to finish off the war with the Parthians. Ventidius had won the battle of Gindarus, and received the Parthian leader's head as a trophy. He was now besieging Samosata, because the king of Commagene, Antiochus, would not release the Parthians sheltering there. Antony took over in late summer, and Ventidius went back to Rome to celebrate a well-earned triumph. He never resumed his military career after that, and died quite soon. It was said that he had accepted bribes from Antiochus and had consequently failed to push the siege of Samosata to its conclusion. For this reason it was thought that he had fallen out with Antony and been disgraced, but if that was the case it is unlikely that Antony would have allowed him to hold a triumph. The most likely explanation is that Ventidius was tired and worn out. He was some years older than Antony. His family had chosen the wrong side in the so-called Social War of 90, and as a child he had been marched through the streets of Rome in the triumph of Pompeius Strabo, the father of Pompey the Great. He must have been at least 55 years old by the time he started the campaign against the Parthians — not an advanced age even by Roman standards, but he had experienced hardships in his youth. It is not very surprising that he did not go back to the east, and the preposterous stories that Antony had him killed can be laid at the door of scandal mongers who wanted to blacken Antony's name. Ventidius' triumph was a nice touch on Antony's part. It served to demonstrate to the Romans that Antony was enjoying rather better success against his enemies and was therefore a better general than Octavian. It kept Antony before the public eye, and lastly it was for Ventidius' own gratification — the child who had featured in Pompeius Strabo's triumph was now holding a triumph of his own. It was an extravagant expression of 'so there!' writ large for public consumption. Antony had never been in favour of, or favoured by, Pompey or the Pompeian circle. Strabo and his son Pompey the Great were both dead, but there were still many people who would understand the gesture.

The siege of Samosata ended by negotiation. Antony withdrew and went to Athens for the winter until the new campaigning season opened in the spring of 37. He had no reason to be dissatisfied with his achievements in 38, despite the delays caused by Octavian. He chose pro-Roman rulers for some of the eastern states, in the hope of stabilising the area ready for next season's activities. Amyntas was put in command of Galatia, and Pontus was entrusted to Polemo. Cleopatra would have more than a passing interest in noting the names and histories of whoever was to be in command of the cities and states of Asia Minor. There was one further event of which Antony may have taken brief notice; in the early autumn of 38, Octavia gave birth to his daughter Antonia. Perhaps he hoped for a son, or perhaps he did not mind. Cleopatra was probably unmoved; her son by Antony was already two years old, with greater opportunities before him than any Roman daughter. History was to curtail these opportunities for him and increase those of Antony's daughters, but in 38, the future seemed secure for Cleopatra's children.

The next year was a monotonous repeat of frustrations and delays for Antony, mostly the fault of Octavian whose conspicuous lack of success against Sextus Pompey had driven him almost to his knees. Antony collected 300 ships and set sail for Italy. History repeated itself; the town authorities of Brundisium would not allow Antony to enter the harbour, so he took himself off to Tarentum, where Octavian joined him. The treaty arranged there provided for the immediate needs of the war against Sextus, and also for the longer term requirements of the Triumvirs. Antony gave Octavian 120 ships, in return for the promise of 20,000 soldiers when he started the war against Parthia. The Triumvirate had expired at the end of 38, so the two men renewed it, quite simply by declaring that they had done so and then bringing the matter before the people of Rome, who gladly passed the law to ratify their possession of power. The few months between the end of 38 and the agreement reached in 37, when they were technically without any legal powers at all, were glossed over. It is not known whether they dutifully back-dated the renewal of their powers from the end of 38, or began the new term from the date of their meeting early in 37. Specific terminal dates were not mentioned, causing insoluble problems for modern historians. Even the ancient scholars were not certain of the date when the Triumvirate should expire, and offer conflicting stories. Probably Antony and Octavian decided not to complicate their lives any more than was necessary. Clear-cut elucidation of terminal dates or any limitations on power restricted their freedom of action. Antony and Octavian probably decided that they would cross that particular bridge when they came to it.

Since it was too late to begin an eastern campaign by the time these important negotiations were over, Antony went to Antioch in Syria, travelling as far as Corcyra (modern Corfu) with Octavia. From there he sent her back to Rome, rather than risk her health in what was to be a base camp to prepare for war. She was pregnant with her second child by Antony, so if he had taken her to Antioch he would probably still have been cast as an inconsiderate husband. Octavian made great use of this seeming rejection of Octavia, but it was not abnormal at the time, and relations between Antony and his wife may not have been so strained in 37 as Octavian wanted the Roman public to believe. Octavia kept her feelings to herself with admirable restraint, continuing to look

21 Carved head of Octavia. Museo Nazionale delle Terme, Rome.
  Photo David Brearley

after her own children by her first husband, Antony's by Fulvia, and her own two daughters from her new marriage. She was the model of wifely virtue, perhaps from personal choice. Her modest behaviour gave Octavian grounds for whipping up dislike of Antony, but whatever Octavia had done, ranging from extreme decorum to total despair, Octavian would have used it against Antony.

Perhaps Antony realised that he was in a situation where whatever he did his motives would be interpreted badly, so he decided to do as he pleased. Once established at Antioch, he sent Gaius Fonteius Capito to Alexandria to invite Cleopatra to join him. With regard to Octavian he did himself and Cleopatra no favours at all by this action, but the material advantages to be gained from Egypt far outweighed the perpetual niggling, with no advantages at all, from Octavian. When he started to drive the Parthians from the eastern territories Antony did not specifically call upon Cleopatra for assistance, but now that the real campaign was beginning to carry the war into Parthia itself, and he had used up so much of his time and resources in arrangements with Octavian and Sextus, he needed help.

Cleopatra arrived in Antioch in the autumn of 37, and spent the winter with Antony. Apart from the campaigns against the Parthians and in Armenia, they were never parted from each other again, and Antony never returned to Rome. She brought with her the twins Alexander and Cleopatra, acknowledged by Antony, now if not earlier, as his children. Perhaps it was in Antioch that they were given their names Alexander Helios, and Cleopatra Selene, deliberately invoking the deep religious significance of the sun (Helios) and moon (Selene). The names were not just empty symbols in a cheap bid for recognition in the east. The promise of beneficence and protection went with them, in a time of great hope for the future. In Rome, Octavian countered by associating himself with the sun god, Apollo.

In return for whatever assistance she gave to Antony Cleopatra was rewarded by her territorial acquisitions, recreating and augmenting the Empire of the Ptolemies. She knew exactly what she wanted, and why. What she eventually gained was all geared to the enrichment of Egypt and to engendering trade. She gained control of most of the important sea ports and much of their hinterland to the north and east of Egypt, along the coasts of Phoenicia and Syria, where only the ancient ports of Tyre and Sidon remained independent. She also gained the harbours at Hamaxia and Elaeusa Sebaste in Cilicia in what is now southern

Turkey. She encroached on Judaea where Antony installed Herod. Ventidius had sent troops to oust the Parthians from Judaea at the same time as he began to besiege Samosata in 40. Herod gained control by degrees; he was not at first in control of Jerusalem, but when he finally established himself there he named his fortress-palace the Antonia, to show gratitude to Antony.

It is said that Cleopatra's main aim was the complete liquidation of Judaea, because a strong Judaea threatened the prosperity and safety of Egypt. It is also said that she could persuade Antony to do whatever she asked because he was weakness itself when he confronted her. Since she gained only the balsam groves from Herod and levied an annual rent on them, but left Gaza independent as his access to the sea, one of the above statements is not correct. Antony did not grant her all that she asked in 37, but did cede territories which were under Roman control. Alienation of parts of the Roman world were not looked upon kindly by the Romans; he must have known what risks he was taking. On the other hand to have Cleopatra in control of important areas while he marched eastwards into Parthia made it worthwhile to take those risks.

A new era was proclaimed in Egypt from 1 September 37, counting the year to follow as the sixteenth of Cleopatra's reign, and also the first. Attempts have been made to associate this new dating with Caesarion, who was ten years old, or perhaps with a marriage ceremony with Antony. The case for Caesarion is weakened because he was still not included in the official records of government, nor does Antony feature in this way. Michael Grant is surely correct in pointing out that it was the reconstituted Ptolemaic Empire that Cleopatra wished to celebrate, from 37 onwards. The territorial acquisitions were of great importance to her, not for the purposes of displaying her own power, but for the financial and material gains for Egypt. Equal distribution of this wealth was not her aim; the Egyptian peasants still laboured, and it probably did not matter to them in the slightest that they laboured in a strong country, but it mattered very much to Cleopatra.

The postulated marriage of Antony and Cleopatra either now or at any other time is not proven. Antony was already married to Octavia, and so he would be entering into a bigamous association with Cleopatra, at least in the eyes of the Romans. If there was a religious ceremony to celebrate the union of Triumvir and Queen, that held

22 Head of Cleopatra from the Cherchel Museum, Algeria, North Africa. The hair curled in Roman fashion is more flamboyant than Cleopatra's usual style, but the facial features compare favourably with other portraits of her. This sculpture has also been identified with Cleopatra Selene, the daughter of Cleopatra and Antony. Courtesy Agence Nationale d'Archéologie et de Protection des Sites et Monuments Historiques, Algiers

deep significance for the eastern states and especially Egypt, it is not specifically recorded as such. By popular consent Antony as Osiris-Dionysus was the consort of Cleopatra as Isis-Aphrodite, accepted in both the Egyptian and Greek worlds. That was probably as far as it went, but since marriage with a non-Roman was forbidden to Antony, his enemies could make something of the uncertainty of his official relationship to Cleopatra. The only literary reference where Antony stated the case for any official marriage is ambiguous; in response to jibes from Octavian, Antony sent him a coarse soldier's letter, taunting Octavian for his affairs with a few Roman women, and passing off his own relationship with Cleopatra with the phrase *uxor mea est*, which has been variously translated. Sometimes it is interpreted as a question, 'is she my wife?', meaning that they were not married after all, and the affair was just an affair. Some credence is lent to this interpretation, because Antony then asked Octavian 'what does it matter where you get your erections?' as though sex was all there was to his association with Cleopatra. Others have seen it differently, however, taking advantage of the absence in Latin of punctuation marks which would have elucidated the problem. The Latin as it stands says 'she is my wife' thus opening up all sorts of further questions, such as the suggestion that Antony merely regarded her as his wife, or that he really was married to her, according to Egyptian law. In the end the problem is academic. Marriage or no marriage, the two participants were already indisputably and permanently linked.

The combination of Antony and Cleopatra as the main rulers of the eastern territories took Caesar's influence many stages further. Caesar's plans for the Parthian campaign may have involved a contribution from Cleopatra, and he may well have intended to bestow on her the territories that she desired to rebuild the Egyptian realm. He and Antony may even have discussed the campaign in 44, when it was in its formative stages, though the plans then were for Antony to remain in Rome, looking after Caesar's interests. All this changed with the murder of Caesar, bringing Antony to the foreground; he was the senior statesman and general, whose intentions towards Rome could not be described as destructive. He was following in Caesar's footsteps for the greater good of Rome. The potential for bringing back great wealth from Parthia would please the Roman mob, and the trading community was eager to follow the army and establish links with the fabulously wealthy lands reaching all the way to India. Dreams of becoming the new Alexander may have entered Antony's head, but perhaps he was more realistic than that; the conquest of Parthia would suffice for the time being. At the beginning of 36, it looked as though he might succeed. He assembled probably the largest army Rome had ever put into the field, and set off in May.

5. Octavian

The year 36 was an eventful one, disastrous for Antony, and highly successful for Octavian. The Parthian campaign started with high expectations of success, with an able commander and a large well-equipped army assembled at Zeugma, situated to the west of Carrhae, where Crassus met defeat in 53. Antony publicised his campaign, perhaps to make it seem that he was about to launch his attack eastwards from Zeugma, to draw the Parthian army to the west to meet the potential threat. Then he marched northwards by way of Samosata into Armenia where he then turned east and south to descend on Media and Parthia from the north. If the move succeeded it would bring him up behind the Parthians, and then he would be able to roll them up between his troops and the Roman held territories, and hopefully bring the king to terms. The plan was sound, but it depended upon rapid movement and quick successes. Antony dashed for the Median capital Phraaspa, variously rendered in the ancient sources as Phraapa, or Praata. Its location is not certain, only that it blocked the way into Parthia and Antony felt that he had to take it.

In the rapid march to reach it he left most of his heavy siege train behind, under his commander Oppius Statianus, and his ally, king Polemo of Pontus. The Parthians attacked and destroyed the siege train, killed Statianus, and took Polemo prisoner. From then on, the Parthians were behind Antony instead of the other way round. He had to extricate himself and march home, losing many men in the process, but displaying all the supreme qualities as a commander that he possessed in keeping the army together, preventing discipline from crumbling, and warding off attacks. When he reached Armenia, he left his generals Publius Canidius Crassus and Domitius Ahenobarbus to shepherd the army to safety, and rode ahead to Syria to arrange for its reception into winter quarters. At some point he sent a message to Cleopatra to bring supplies, ready cash, and clothing. He established his headquarters at Leuke Come on the Syrian coast between Berytus and Sidon, where he could do nothing very much except wait for her. He drank heavily, and spent hours on the shore, watching for her ships.

Probably in January 35, she arrived. The numbers of ships and the cargoes they carried are not enumerated in the ancient sources. She would have needed some time to gather everything together, relying upon her efficient administration to spur everyone into action. Then she set sail with the squadrons, to meet Antony. She was nearly 35 years old and had just given birth to her fourth child, Antony's son Ptolemy Philadelphus; if for nothing else, she has to be admired for her stamina. Her determination to be in the centre of action also has to be admired. When she sent a fleet to help the Triumvirs against the conspirators, she sailed with it personally, instead of relying upon subordinates, and now she sailed in winter to come to Antony's help. Various interpretations could be placed on her actions. If she trusted no-one except herself to carry out her tasks, she was merely following a course that many other monarchs have found advisable if not vitally necessary. If she wanted to be at the forefront in order to take the credit for successes, she also shouldered the blame for failures. Neglect of her duties as Queen of Egypt was never a charge that could be laid against her. Nor could she neglect her Roman ally and let him lapse into despair, because she needed him to be a powerful force in the east. But in coming to Antony at Leuke Come she combined all these roles with a normal human emotion.

Her voyage to Antony at the beginning of 35 permanently sealed her association with him, and ultimately started them both on final stages of the road to war with Octavian and their final defeat. She was probably perspicacious enough to realise that in Rome Octavian was gaining ground rapidly. In September 36, he won the naval battle of Naulochus, driving Sextus from the Mediterranean. Octavian himself was the figure head and the facilitator, while his friend Marcus Vipsanius Agrippa carried out the fighting and won the battles. Agrippa had spent many months training his crews in naval warfare on an artificially deepened lake before he even ventured to bring Sextus to battle. He had studied form and analysed previous mistakes, and did not emerge until he was ready. Perhaps preoccupied with the disastrous retreat from Parthia, and the sorry condition of their soldiers, Antony and Cleopatra failed to take serious notice of the abilities and experience of Marcus Vipsanius Agrippa in naval warfare.

An event which must have given both of them some pause for thought was the elimination of Lepidus as a partner in the Triumvirate. From Africa Lepidus had sailed to Octavian's assistance against Sextus Pompey, but once established in Sicily he staged a short-lived attempt to assume power for himself. Octavian made short work of him, sparing his life but depriving him of political influence and personal freedom. He also took over Lepidus' province of Africa, thus bringing the rich corn-growing province under his control, with more troops at his disposal. Lepidus survived until 12 BC, still in office as Pontifex Maximus, but with no powers whatsoever and no hope of gaining any. He was unable to play a part ever again in the political arena. When he died, Octavian, who was by then Augustus, took over his priestly office. The elimination of Lepidus left Octavian and Antony, still called Triumvirs though there were now only two of them, to share power. Their relationship was fragile, but compared to other anxious political crises witnessed in Rome, it was amicable enough. Antony was still the senior partner, with more military experience and greater resources.

It may seem that if only Cleopatra had been ruthless enough she could have abandoned Antony as he waited for her in Syria, refused to come to his assistance, and changed her allegiance. Octavian's star was rising, but it is only historical hindsight that lends such importance to Octavian's successes in 36. In order to gain military credit to match Antony's standing, he was also planning to follow up his victory over Sextus with a campaign in the difficult mountainous territory of Illyricum, against traditionally aggressive tribes who posed no direct threat to Rome, except that they blocked routes from northern Italy and the Danube to Greece and the south. It is easy to forget that Octavian still had a very long way to go before he won sole power for himself, and could have lost his political influence at any time before, or even after, the battle of Actium.

At the beginning of 35 Cleopatra would not see Octavian as a potential ally or as a prop for her personal power. In any case she was never free to act solely on a personal basis. She was Egypt personified, and Egypt was part of the east, and Antony, the foremost Roman general of the era, had been given control of the east. She had formed a strong liaison with him that committed her and Egypt to his policies, which were in an advanced formative stage, and depended mostly on Antony himself, acting on behalf of Rome. The old Republican days of magistrates, governors and generals appointed by lot or by election, going out to their provinces or to the wars, reporting dutifully back to the Senate, supposedly with no personal interest in long-term commands and wide ranging powers, had gone forever and could not return. Antony was Cleopatra's inevitable choice. If he had been killed while retreating from Parthia through the snows of Armenia, Cleopatra would have experienced some tense moments, whilst waiting, fully alert, for the outcome of such a disaster. It is difficult to decide who could have filled Antony's role at that point. Canidius Crassus would have been able to rally the army, but he did not have the political standing at Rome to take over where Antony left off. Cleopatra would have been forced to concentrate on Egypt, garnering strength and probably fighting to keep her territorial acquisitions. The eastern states would have squabbled amongst themselves, and some of them would hope to extricate themselves from her control; they would look to the only other bright light in the Roman heavens, Octavian, whose happy knack of seizing opportunities would have brought him to world power that much sooner.

Though some authors portray Antony as hopelessly lost from this point onwards, he was not the pathetic figure portrayed in Augustan propaganda. His appointments of pro-Roman eastern rulers and the strengthening of the various kingdoms was still sound, and though he had failed to inflict on Parthia the crushing defeat that he had aspired to, such a conquest was not entirely out of the question, and Antony was still the man to stabilise, and as far as possible, unify the east. He needed Cleopatra's support to do it, so she gave it willingly for the next campaign in 34, against Armenia.

During 35, Antony made no move. He needed time to recuperate, and so did the army. He had lost valuable equipment and supplies, which had to be refurbished, and he would also need to formulate another plan to redress the balance of his losses. On the political front in 35, Antony had to deal with Sextus Pompey who had escaped to the east after the battle of Naulochus, offering to ally with Antony. Nothing was concluded, perhaps because Antony realised that an alliance with Sextus would only compromise him. When Sextus began to intrigue with the Parthians, showing that he could not be trusted, Antony despatched his general Titius to bring him to terms, hoping to spare his life if he could be pinned down to some permanent agreement. He could not. Instead of negotiating, Sextus attacked and burned some of Titius' ships, and met his end by execution. Munatius

Plancus, the governor of Asia Minor and Syria, possibly gave the final order, but behind him there was the power of Antony, who probably took no pleasure at all in ridding the Roman world of the man who had been a thorn in its side for many years. Thus the younger son of Pompey the Great met his end.

Whilst Antony was not the irresolute failure depicted in the later sources, he seems to have reached a turning point in 35. Just as Cleopatra had placed herself irrevocably at his side, he chose to demonstrate that his future lay in the east and not with Octavian in the west. He broke off relations with his wife Octavia in very public fashion. In normal circumstances he would have wintered at Athens, or if his campaign was getting started, at Antioch. But in 35 he stayed in Alexandria. Octavia came to Athens with money, supplies and troops, though not the full complement of 20,000 men that he had been promised at Tarentum by Octavian. She was a good wife to Antony, she was the mother of his two daughters, and she looked after all his other offspring as though they were her own. Totally blameless, she was rejected by Antony, who instructed her to send on the supplies and the troops, but to go back home herself. His reasons are open to question, and it is natural that Cleopatra should be blamed as 'the other woman', albeit a very illustrious one, for encouraging Antony to break off relations with his wife. On an emotional level there may have been an element of jealousy, but that is less likely and less important than the wider political implications of Antony's actions. His marriage with Octavia was not a match made in heaven; it was a political alliance of the kind that leading Romans entered into all the time. Women were the political pawns in the shifting allegiances between ruling Roman magnates; if they were very lucky they loved their husbands and were loved by them in return, much as Pompey and Caesar's daughter Julia were said to have fallen in love with each other. Some women were unlucky and consequently they led miserable lives, but most of them would experience the middle ground, with households of their own, access to money and even some influence over their husbands.

Antony's treatment of Octavia was not as heartless as it has been described. It would be another three years before he finally divorced her, and even then it was not such an abnormal procedure in the power-play of ancient Rome, no matter how successful the marriage had been. Caesar divorced one of his wives to avoid a scandal, Pompey divorced his wife when he came back from the east, and then he married Julia, rearranging his family alliances to gain his own ends. Octavian married Scribonia, a relative of Sextus Pompey, for purely political ends, and then when the time came to break with Sextus, he divorced her on the same day that she gave birth to his daughter Julia. There was no public outcry then about Octavian's heartless treatment of his virtuous wife. The most significant factor in Antony's rejection of Octavia in 35 is that he was ready to break off close relations with Octavian, for reasons which can only be surmised, and the most significant factor about what Octavian made of it is that he used it to portray Cleopatra as the evil Queen who had set out to destroy Rome.

After his fallow period in 35, Antony began to prepare the foundations for another campaign in the east. During the march to Phraaspa in the previous year the Armenian allies under their king Artavasdes had deserted Antony. The alliance was a shaky one to start with, and the Armenian troops were not really interested in this Roman war. Artavasdes was in a difficult position, morally and territorially, sandwiched as he was between the two largest and greatest Empires of the ancient world. Antony had not been able to make any demonstration of strength against him while he retreated through Armenia in 36, though the soldiers made it clear that in their opinion a punitive expedition should be mounted. In 34 Antony re-opened negotiations, testing the waters. He sent Dellius as his envoy, suggesting a marriage alliance between the five year old Alexander Helios and the infant daughter of Artavsades. Together Rome and Armenia could campaign against the Parthian king Phraates, who at that moment was preoccupied with rebellions in his court circle. There was a further advantage in that the king of Media, also named Artavasdes, had suddenly turned against Phraates and offered to ally with Rome. Only Armenia now stood in the way of a clear passage into Parthia.

There was no response from the Armenian Artavasdes. Having offered the peaceful alternative to persuade him to enter into an alliance with Rome, Antony adopted an aggressive attitude and mobilised for an invasion. Cleopatra accompanied him from Egypt through Syria as far as the Euphrates. The settlement of Armenia was a vital preliminary to entering into a Parthian war, and it seems that Antony succeeded in the task of annexing and pacifying it. Artavasdes was taken prisoner, Armenia was garrisoned, and Canidius Crassus was placed in command of the troops when Antony returned to Alexandria.

Traders began to establish themselves in the Armenian kingdom. The scene was set for occupation and the use of Armenia as a springboard for a descent on Parthia. Antony's coins proclaiming that Armenia had been conquered (ARMENIA DEVICTA) were based on reality, and not on empty bluster, though Octavian dismissed his achievements as an expensive tantrum for the sake of revenging himself on Artavasdes for not supporting him in the campaign of 36.

When she parted from Antony at the Euphrates, Cleopatra went on a Royal progress through her expanded Empire. On the journey back to Egypt, she came by way of Damascus to call on Herod, recently established as ruler of Judaea. He received her regally as befitted the Queen of Egypt, and the acknowledged mistress, if not the wife, of Antony. Herod could not afford to upset his powerful Roman supporter, but from his own account, preserved at third hand in the pages of the Jewish writer Flavius Josephus, Cleopatra's visit set his teeth on edge. Herod's memoirs have not survived into modern times, but what he wrote was used by Nicolaus of Damascus in his historical works, which were in turn relayed to the ancient world in the first century AD by Josephus. Nicolaus had been engaged by Cleopatra as the tutor of her children, and presumably travelled with her and Alexander Helios and Cleopatra Selene as she journeyed southwards through Syria and Judaea. He must have been impressed by Herod, because he found employment with him after Cleopatra's death, not as tutor this time but as adviser. He went on to associate himself with Octavian-Augustus, and wrote a eulogistic biography of him. These later associations cast a dubious light on what Nicolaus wrote about Cleopatra, firstly because his employer and benefactor Herod had no reason to like the Queen who encroached on his kingdom, and secondly Augustus never relented from his profound enmity towards her. It was not possible to write glowingly of the young Octavian and then to write sympathetically about Cleopatra. By the time that Flavius Josephus began to write, the image of Cleopatra as the most vicious, scheming and powerful enemy Rome ever faced was crystallised and indissoluble.

The activities of Antony and Cleopatra in the summer of 34 gave Octavian every opportunity to turn the Roman people against them. After the conclusion of the Armenian campaign, Antony staged a procession through the streets of Alexandria that so closely emulated a Roman triumph that it seemed malicious, even sacrilegious, since all

23 A silver coin (denarius) of 32, with the heads of Antony and Cleopatra. This coin is a very important piece of evidence for the political developments in Alexandria in the years before the civil war with Octavian. It conveys definite statements of achievements and intentions. Antony's message (ANTONI. ARMENIA. DEVICTA) declares that he has conquered Armenia. Later sources, influenced by Augustan propaganda, claimed that the campaign was a fiasco and nothing was achieved, but Antony was deeply involved in the civil war with Octavian before he had time to consolidate his conquests. A Roman garrison was installed in Armenia, the king Artavasdes was captured and brought to Alexandria, and Roman traders began to do business in Armenia, all of which lead to the conclusion that the campaign was successful. Antony's claims to conquest can be allowed to stand and taken at face value. Cleopatra's message declares that she is Queen of kings and of her sons who are kings (CLEOPATRAE REGINAE REGUM FILIORUM REGUM). This is very much a statement of her current position as overlord of the vast territories assigned to her by Antony at the ceremony known as the Donations of Alexandria, and it is also a declaration of intent that she would be succeeded by her children. Her portrait is scarcely flattering. She looks more masculine than she does on her other coins, and it has been pointed out that with the passage of time she and Antony began to look very similar on their coinage. It was probably a deliberate policy on the part of Antony and Cleopatra, to portray themselves as equals in power and achievements. © British Museum

spoils of war were supposed to be dedicated to the chief of the Roman gods, Jupiter Optimus Maximus, in his temple on the Capitol. Cleopatra watched the procession with Caesarion at her side. Reports reaching Rome would be magnified out of all proportion as to her arrogant presumption, and it would also seem as though Antony intended to dedicate the spoils of his conquests to her, and not to the Roman gods. His next actions only served to strengthen this judgement of him. Following closely on the triumphal procession, Antony arranged a second ceremony, now commonly known as the Donations of Alexandria. He and Cleopatra sat enthroned before a large crowd with the children seated on smaller thrones in front of them, while all the Royal family received large territories from Antony, some of which were not yet conquered, and some of which were not strictly in Antony's gift. Armenia, Media and Parthia were to be the kingdom of Alexander Helios, even though Parthia was still independent, and Media was an allied state. Cleopatra Selene's kingdom was somewhat less fanciful, comprising Cyrenaica and Libya to the west of Egypt, and Ptolemy Philadelphus, not yet three years old, was granted Syria and Cilicia.

Caesarion had always been marked out as the successor to the throne of Egypt, and Antony unequivocally confirmed this position. He also confirmed Caesarion's Roman inheritance as the heir of Caesar. As far as Antony was concerned, he had never doubted the boy's paternity, and had been prepared to testify to that effect in public, but at this juncture there was much more weight behind his affirmation, since he acknowledged Cleopatra's dominion over most of the east, and by dint of that he implied that Caesarion too was to be the successor to this exalted position. On his coins proclaiming the victory over Armenia, Antony showed the head of Cleopatra, in no flattering portrayal as she stares, hatchet-faced, hook-nosed and frowning, encircled by the legend running round the coin 'CLEOPATRAE REGINAE REGUM FILIORUM REGUM', 'to Cleopatra, Queen of kings and her sons who are kings'. The Donations of Alexandria were serious in intent, to recreate and augment the Ptolemaic Empire, with Cleopatra and her children as its rulers. Just as Cleopatra was Queen of kings, so one day Caesarion would be King of kings. Octavian was under no real threat from the boy Caesarion as the son and heir of Caesar, nor as the Ptolemaic ruler of Egypt, nor even from Caesarion in both these roles. But Caesarion as eventual overlord of the east from Cyrenaica to Syria and from Egypt to Cilicia, with command over his brothers and his sister, and access to huge resources, posed a different, more serious, threat. It would be rather better to ensure that such a situation never materialised.

Cleopatra was now in a much stronger position than ever before, with Antony's armies to back her up, and after the success of the Armenian campaign, it seemed likely that Parthia might possibly be conquered too. That would give Antony and Cleopatra a preponderant influence in the east, which was being steadily unified under their control. It would also bring tremendous kudos for Antony in Rome. Parthia was the old enemy, and so endless laurels, praise and political advantage would accrue to the man who conquered it. As the year closed, Antony was poised to restart the Parthian campaign in 33, using Armenia as a base.

In that same year, the Triumvirate would expire. The problem of the exact date when the powers of the Triumvirs ran out has exercised scholars for many years, and will probably never be satisfactorily resolved. When Octavian and Antony reached agreement at Tarentum in 37, technically they held no powers at all, since the first five-year term of the Triumvirate had already ended. There is some support for the argument that the second five-year term of the Triumvirate was backdated to pick up where the first term left off, because in his brief account of his reign, the *Res Gestae Divi Augusti*, Augustus declared that he had been Triumvir for ten consecutive years, as though there had been no embarrassing and anomalous gap in his powers, during which it could be said that he had acted without legality. On the other hand the historian Appian says that the second term of the Triumvirate ended in 32.

The precise date cannot be established, but in the end perhaps it is less important than the political attitudes of the two contestants for power. Before there could be any controversy about the Triumvirate, Octavian pre-empted criticism by ceasing to use the title, while Antony continued to do so. By his defeat of Sextus and then his military activities in Illyricum, Octavian had paved the way to fame and glory in Rome, and in 33 he and Agrippa embarked on a civic regeneration programme in Rome, attending to crumbling buildings, inspecting and renewing the sewers, and founding new shrines and temples. The old Roman virtues were praised and revived, for their unifying character and also as a backcloth on which to highlight the non-Roman activities of Antony and especially the foreign Queen Cleopatra.

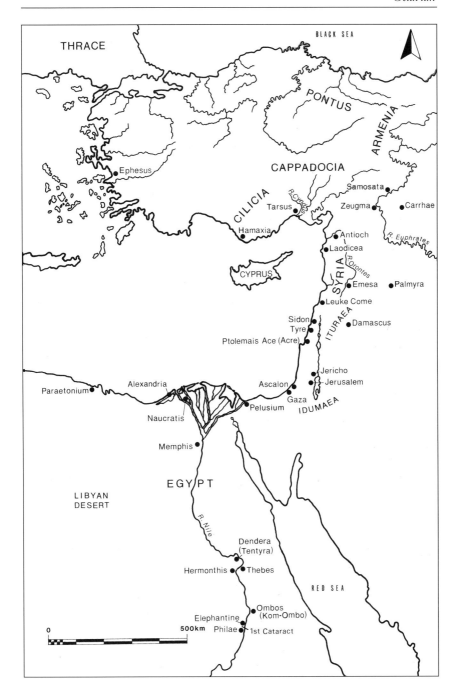

24 *Map of Egypt and the eastern provinces, showing places mentioned in the text.*
Cleopatra revived the old Ptolemaic Empire, acquiring control of ports and harbours
and profitable lands with the assistance of Antony. Drawn by Graeme Stobbs

It was on Cleopatra that Octavian began to focus. Antony still had supporters in Rome and Italy, and Octavian could not attack him directly because he had no real grounds for hostility. It would have been a forlorn hope to try to instigate another civil war, this time against a strong Roman general who had not yet done Rome any irreparable harm. But the time was fast approaching when Octavian would have to find some other path to power without resorting to an arrangement such as the Triumvirate. He was determined not to lapse into a subordinate role to Antony, who was probably about to succeed in conquering Parthia, and would be unbearably popular in both Rome and the east when he returned victorious, bringing in his wake vast wealth, tribute and opportunities to extend Roman trading activities to the distant eastern lands. The other options to this unwelcome subordinate position were equality with Antony, superiority to him, or eradication of him as a potent force. Octavian was consul in 33, and beginning to feel secure. He had been granted the sacrosanctity of the tribunes as a reward for his defeat of Sextus Pompey in 36, an important privilege that he preserved all through his reign as Augustus. Blaming Cleopatra for the malign influence she had over Antony, Octavian launched his campaign against her in a speech in the Senate in 33. He dragged out all the usual accusations that Antony's eastern sympathies, his lack of self-control, his un-Roman behaviour, his supposed failures in military conquests, could all be laid at the door of the scheming Egyptian Queen who was obviously aiming for world domination, and in the process the destruction of Rome.

25 *Head of Cleopatra from the Berlin Antikensammlung, carved in the classical tradition.* © *Berlin Museen*

6. Actium

Antony seemed to be unaware that in Rome his reputation was steadily being eroded. He continued with his plans for the conquest of Parthia, so for most of 33 the larger part of his army was in Armenia, where it remained until the autumn. Some scholars dispute the date of Octavian's first speech denouncing Antony and Cleopatra, preferring to place it not in his consulship in 33, but in 32 when preparations for the civil war were well advanced. This different dating exonerates Octavian of all guilt, implying that it was Antony and Cleopatra who prepared for war before Octavian had declared his enmity openly, and that therefore Octavian was the innocent, injured party. It is unlikely that Octavian waited until 32 to start proceedings, because in 33 Antony was going from strength to strength, and about to embark on the most important external war that Rome could ever undertake. Octavian would be overshadowed, and would have to find some way of keeping himself in the public eye. Just as Pompey had always contrived to save the state in its hour of need, Octavian had to find a way of making himself indispensable to Rome so that unrivalled power would be given to him freely, willingly and without hindrance, at least until the crisis was over. It would be wise to begin proceedings in this direction while he was consul, in a fully legal office. To engage in agitation directed against Antony after he ceased to be consul would look like sour grapes, and if he had no magistracy not only would he be powerless but he would have no official voice of his own, and would be forced to address the Senate on his own account as a private individual, or at second hand via another mouthpiece. In those circumstances his arguments would be blunted. He took it upon himself while he was consul to point out the terrible dangers that awaited Rome from the direction of the east, and then he let his audience come to the conclusion that he was the very person to deal with these dangers.

During 33, personal and official communications between Antony in Armenia and Octavian in Rome became more abusive, with Antony pointing out, quite rightly, that he had not received his promised 20,000 soldiers in return for the 120 ships he had given to Octavian. He also raised the question of his veteran soldiers, who did not seem to be quite so favoured as Octavian's in the land settlements in Italy and elsewhere, and allegedly he laid claim to half of Sicily, which Octavian had taken over after Sextus was driven out of it and Lepidus tried to make his stand. Antony put in a word in favour of Lepidus, demanding fairer treatment for him, but it was too late. Octavian merely replied that he was willing to share Sicily, if Antony would share Armenia.

Next, Octavian reproached Antony for his relationship with Cleopatra, and his elevation of Caesarion, which drew from Antony the famous letter reproduced in Suetonius' life of Augustus. Antony pointed out that Octavian went to bed with whoever he chose, so what was the difference if he slept with Cleopatra? The controversial phrase '*uxor mea est*' has already been mentioned; some authors have chosen to interpret this phrase as a question, with the unspoken meaning that 'it does not matter what I do since I am not married to her'. But the words as they stand are not unequivocal; if Antony had wanted to say that she was not his wife, the Latin language was perfectly equipped with simple words like *non* with which to express negative ideas. Either Antony meant to convey that he was married to Cleopatra, or perhaps more likely that he regarded her as his wife. He knew perfectly well that marriage with a foreigner was forbidden by Roman law, and that he was still legally married to Octavia, so his apologists maintain that he must have employed the phrase as a question, meaning 'is she my wife after all?' But that is more tortuous than is really necessary. The truth is perhaps more damning in ancient Roman eyes, in that Antony and Cleopatra probably saw themselves as far above the ordinary laws, and not bound by such mundane considerations. At any rate, Antony and Cleopatra were now a single entity, whether they were married or not.

That was convenient for Octavian. If Cleopatra had not existed, and if Antony had been independent, merely allied to whoever happened to be the ruler of Egypt and drawing money and supplies from his alliance, but not personally associated with that ruler, then Octavian would have had to invent some plausible excuse for making war on him. The supposition that the war would never have started but for Cleopatra is not valid. Eventually the two most powerful men in Rome would have reached the conclusion that it would be better if there were only one of them to direct where Rome went next. Octavian perhaps saw further ahead and began to plan for this eventuality sooner than Antony did. Cleopatra was a gift from the gods to Octavian. He used her as a lever to prise Antony from his position of power, and then when it was all over he assumed even more power for himself, but under a different guise. Without Cleopatra he would not have been able to do it so successfully. He could not have stopped Antony in 33 simply by denouncing the Parthian campaign, since Caesar himself had planned one, and Romans in general would never understand why one of their own politicians, especially one related to Caesar in such an incontrovertible manner, would speak against it. Nor could Octavian sit back and wait for the Parthians to annihilate Antony, just as they had annihilated Crassus. This time they might not succeed. If Antony won and came back victorious, Octavian would have to exert tremendous energy to remain supreme. He had already waged a war against the recalcitrant tribes of Illyricum, and Agrippa had carried Roman arms through Gaul and across the Rhine, emulating and even surpassing Caesar. That was all in the past now and in danger of being forgotten. Without a military command the road to the top was that much more difficult and infinitely slower, and subject to so many hazards. A massive onslaught against Antony offered all sorts of advantages. It would legitimise Octavian's command of troops, and if he won the war he could think of some way of remaining in control; if he lost he could perhaps conclude some bargain with Antony, then lie low and wait for better times. The risks were great, but the potential rewards were greater.

In November 33 Antony abandoned the plans for the Parthian campaign and ordered Canidius to bring the troops out of Armenia. War with Octavian was inevitable, and would require a different set of preparations than a war against a foreign enemy. Antony attended to his legions, issuing a famous series of coins featuring each legion in turn. The soldiers needed careful treatment in order to persuade them to fight the armies of another Roman leader. The reasons why they were being asked to do so would need to be more clearly outlined than they would against a foreign enemy; this was where Octavian had the advantage because he was able to persuade the Romans that they were going to war against the Queen of Egypt, whose intentions towards Rome were not benign. He insinuated that it was unfortunate that

26 Antony's legionary coinage was issued in 31 to honour all his legions individually. This coin shows the standards of the Seventh legion on the reverse, and on the obverse spreads the message that Antony was still Triumvir. The Triumvirate expired probably in 32, though the date is much disputed, and Octavian ceased to use the title before it expired, both to pre-empt criticism and remain politically correct. The coin also shows a Roman war galley, acknowledging the splendid fleet that Antony had assembled with a large contribution of men, money and ships from Cleopatra. At this stage, neither Antony nor Cleopatra could know how significant the fleet was to be in the war against Octavian. © British Museum

Antony had to be sacrificed as well, but as everyone could clearly see, Antony was so deeply embedded in Egyptian ideology and so bewitched by Cleopatra that there was nothing that could be done to save him. If he was not sacrificed, then Octavian could not be held responsible for the consequences. He would need only to remind the Romans that one of Cleopatra's reported remarks, uttered quite frequently, was 'When I dispense justice on the Capitol'. Whether or not this was true did not matter. Romans would be convinced that Cleopatra aimed to dominate the whole world, and therefore she had to be stopped. Rumour would be worth any amount of recruitment posters or hard-bitten centurions touring the country to spread the word that army life was good for you and brought substantial rewards.

Antony's task was more difficult because he was far from Rome, and his generals had not been seen in triumphal parades quite so often as Octavian's, and in any case, he had been left behind in the self-advertising power-play. Octavian and Agrippa had moved on; they had by-passed triumphs, making them seem outmoded by a kind of inverted snobbery where on occasion they refused to hold them even if they were offered by the Senate, maintaining that what they did was not for the greater glory of their persons, but for Rome. It was the Senate that Antony needed to win over. He had already obtained approval for all his arrangements in the east, both past and future, while he was in Rome in October 39, but now he asked again. Cleopatra's position as ruler of large parts of the east had not figured prominently in his schemes in 39, but by 33 Egypt and its ruler was the linchpin of his eastern administrative system. Recognising that the time had come for a major revision of his powers, which had either expired or were about to come to and end, he offered to lay down the Triumviral office — if Octavian would do the same. This was a repeat of the wrangling between Pompey and Caesar, in which Antony as tribune had played a part towards the outbreak of the civil war in 49. He cannot have failed to make a comparison with the two former magnates offering to lay down their commands if the other would comply, but in those days, Pompey and Caesar had not reached such lofty, all-embracing powers as their successors. Antony was upstaged even in this offer, because while he had still used the title Triumvir on his coins and in his proclamations, Octavian had tacitly ceased to use it at all, though in reality he still wielded all the force he required without the Triumviral title.

Octavian ensured that Antony had little time to do very much more to win over the Senate. The consuls for 32 were committed Antonians, Gaius Sosius and Domitius Ahenobarbus, so in theory Antony ought to have been able to redress the balance between Octavian's increasing popularity and his own waning influence via the two chief magistrates in Rome. The year began well when Sosius delivered a speech denouncing Octavian. What he said is not known, but his speech probably contained a catalogue of Octavian's mistreatment of his erstwhile ally and fellow Triumvir, and perhaps countered all the charges laid against Antony with perfectly plausible arguments. Octavian was not present to hear the speech, so there was no reply from him that day. It seemed as though Antony might bring over reasonable-minded people to his side. Sosius wound up his speech by a proposal which the tribune Nonius Balbus vetoed. What was proposed is not known. Assuredly, whatever it was, it would not have been to Octavian's advantage, but it may have fallen short of asking the Senate to declare him an enemy of the state. Nonius may have acted on his own initiative, or he may have been in Octavian's pay. No-one knows for certain.

Losing no time, Octavian resorted to dramatics, decidedly not amateur, but undoubtedly illegal. At the next session of the Senate, he brought a bodyguard with him, and sat coolly between the two consuls. This was unprecedented, and quite out of order, but the enormity of it all was totally eclipsed when Octavian announced that he had proof, in documentary form, that would condemn Antony. He offered to bring this document, or documents, to the next meeting. If he did possess such proof, he was never asked to produce it. The senators took him at his word. The two consuls and many of their colleagues packed their bags and made a dash for Antony's winter headquarters at Ephesus, where he was staying with Cleopatra. It was as simple as that, but as with most simple results, there had been a lot of quiet groundwork before it came to fruition. Men do not flee their homes and go to war in another country far away on a sudden whim; there will have been an increasing awareness of dangerous undercurrents in political life long before Octavian placed his chair between those of the consuls.

The story goes that 300 senators came over to Antony, but the figure is a modern interpretation. The only firmly attested figure is the 700 senators who remained with Octavian, according to Augustus' statement in the *Res Gestae* written at the end of his reign. The Senate had supposedly been augmented by Julius Caesar, who adlected many new men to its ranks, so the new total had risen to about 1000 members. The 700 senators who sided with Octavian, subtracted from the alleged total, leaves 300 to flee to Antony, but there is no proof for this figure. The important statistic is that over twice as many supported Octavian, a fact that Octavian-Augustus did not have to outline in quite so many words.

All hope of a peaceful outcome to the preliminary manoeuvring came to an end when Antony divorced Octavia in 32. Whether or not Cleopatra urged him to do so is not known, but she was probably secure enough in her relationship with Antony to ignore the finer details of his Roman marriage. The divorce was a political statement, and it perhaps precipitated a realignment of loyalties among leading Romans, who would begin to pay minutely detailed attention to their longer-term futures. The two men who had been instrumental in executing Sextus Pompey, Titius and Munatius Plancus, deserted Antony to go to Octavian with important information. Their reasons for this decision are not clear, but there are no lack of accusations that they could not tolerate Cleopatra, so they left because she had too much influence over Antony. It may have been because they saw that Octavian was using her as the excuse to make war, and perhaps also they judged it very likely that he would win, because Antony's troops were not so keen to fight what could only be a civil war, as Octavian's were to fight what they had been told was a foreign one.

The information that Titius and Plancus brought was that Antony had made his will and lodged it as was normal with the Vestals in their temple. Such documents were meant to be private and protected, but Octavian obtained it, opened it in private, and then read the contents to the Senate. No-one pointed out that this was very irregular; all of Rome was too busy expressing shock that Antony affirmed Cleopatra as ruler of the territories he had granted to her, and further that Antony also affirmed that Caesarion was the son of Caesar and would inherit the vast domains that Cleopatra ruled. Finally, and most scandalously, Antony's wishes were that they should be buried side by side in their beloved Alexandria. If Octavian invented all this, or even forged a will purporting to be Antony's, what he said he had found in it was very plausible, based on previous experience and Antony's own actions. Seemingly no-one in the Senate stood up to declare disbelief. It was taken for granted that Antony had severed his allegiance to Rome for ever. If that was the case, perhaps he would eventually turn against her, and try to convert the west into an eastern and mainly Egyptian dependency. He might try to make Alexandria into the capital of the world, with Cleopatra as Queen. It carried no weight whatsoever that Egypt had developed a highly-sophisticated civilisation several centuries before Romulus built a few huts by the Tiber. Cleopatra was the enemy. There had to be war. Octavian sat back while people cried out for it. Just to make sure, he engineered an oath of loyalty to himself as leader in this war, so that later he could proclaim that the whole of Italy and the western provinces were united behind him. The significant point is that this oath was sworn to him as leader. In more normal times it would have been sworn to Rome, or at least to the Senate and people of Rome. Autocracy lurked in the wings, waiting to walk onto centre-stage, but no-one noticed, or cared. There was a larger threat from Cleopatra. All that remained was to declare war in proper Roman fashion. Octavian discovered an antiquated and picturesque ceremonial that appealed to the heightened mood in

Rome. The ritual consisted of marking out a piece of ground and designating it as enemy territory, then casting a spear into it as war was declared.

In response Antony did not even consider an invasion of Italy, with all the difficulties of crossing the sea, fighting his way up to Rome and then establishing control. He would have been in an adverse position to begin with if he bludgeoned his way to power, striding his way across thousands of Italian and Roman corpses to set himself up as — what? He himself had abolished the Dictatorship after the murder of Caesar. The Triumvirate was a dead letter. The consulship as an annual office was not sufficient to allow him to achieve all that would be necessary when he arrived in Rome. If, on the other hand, he could beat off and survive an aggressive attack by Octavian, he could start more slowly and perhaps maintain himself in Rome without arousing too much antagonism. He decided to stay in the east, which he knew well, and which knew him. Most eastern kings and princes had some association with him, and could be expected to help him defend their home territories, whereas he could not hope to carry them with him in an invasion of Italy, where they would be unwelcome whether they were victorious or not.

He chose Greece as his battleground, and went to Patrae for the winter of 32–31. The first consideration was to patrol the seas and guard the coast, to stop Octavian from landing and gaining a foothold. With 500 ships Antony could hope to carry out the former task of patrolling the Adriatic and part of the Mediterranean sea, but the long coast of Greece, made even longer by the number of inlets and bays, was impossible to close up, despite the fact that he had many ships, several legions and additional units of native levies with which to do it. The largest contingents of troops were based near the Gulf of Ambracia, where the bay of Actium sheltered his ships.

Cleopatra remained with Antony throughout the campaign. Details are lost, because in the surviving sources the emphasis is on Octavian's successes and not on anything that Antony achieved. What has come down to us is the tradition that the army in general objected to Cleopatra, and wanted Antony to send her back to Egypt, but there was at least one voice in her defence, a voice which had considerable influence by dint of the speaker's experience and his proven loyalty to Antony. Canidius Crassus pointed out that Cleopatra was paying the troops and providing a large part of the supplies, and that to send her

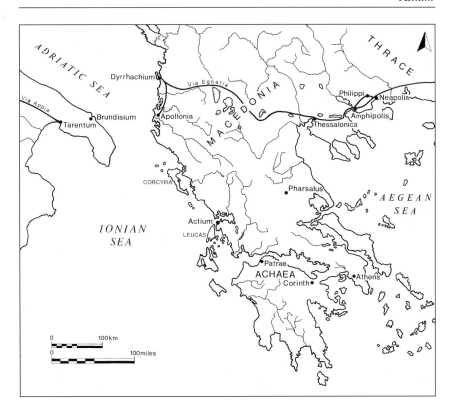

27 *Map of Greece, showing places mentioned in the text. Antony was a confirmed Graecophile, studying at Athens in his youth, and wintering there on more than one occasion. He fought two major campaigns in Greece, the first with Caesar against Pompey, ending with the battle of Pharsalus, and the second with Octavian, culminating in the battle of Philippi. In 31 when he was blockaded at Actium, his choices were to retreat inland as Canidius Crassus advocated, or to try to break the blockade and make for the open sea as Cleopatra advised. The sea voyage to Egypt was so much more easily accomplished than an overland march through the various eastern territories, and once there, Antony and Cleopatra could rebuild their armies and reassemble what was left of their fleet. Drawn by Graeme Stobbs*

back to Alexandria would alienate the Egyptian contingents, who manned many of the ships. He went on to praise Cleopatra herself. He said that in his opinion she was equally as intelligent as any other king who took part in the war, and that since she had managed a large kingdom without assistance for many years and had learned a great deal from Antony, she should be invited to remain at headquarters. It may be that Plutarch, who reports this episode in his life of Antony, used Canidius as a credible mouthpiece to put across his own point of view about Cleopatra; it was after all a recognised ploy of ancient authors to dramatise in this way in order to present different opinions of people and events. But Canidius does emerge as a balanced personality from his constant reliability before Actium and his dogged loyalty afterwards. It was suggested that Cleopatra must have bribed him to make his speech, a charge which is probably without foundation. Firstly she was quite capable of making her own speech to defend her position, and secondly, if Canidius could be bribed to say something that he did not necessarily believe, then he would just as casually have been able to accept bribes from Octavian, without troubling his conscience. When Canidius was trying to march the army back to Alexandria after Antony and Cleopatra sailed away from Actium, the troops went over to Octavian on the promise of a large donative, but Canidius himself refused to accept money, and marched on. It is very likely that Canidius did say what Plutarch reports of him, and he was perhaps more persuasive than Domitius Ahenobarbus, who advocated sending Cleopatra away. It was rumoured that even the troops shared his viewpoint, and offered to rid themselves of Antony and follow Ahenobarbus as leader instead. Some short time later, when he was already very ill, Ahenobarbus deserted to Octavian. Perhaps he did not object to Cleopatra herself, but to the propaganda value that she represented to Octavian. It would have been so much less murky and complicated if Antony fought entirely on his own account, without the Queen of Egypt.

The confidence of Antony's troops was eroded when Agrippa launched a naval attack on the most important of the Antonian harbours at Methone in south-western Greece, and it fell to him quite quickly. This meant that Octavian's ships had a base of operations, and Agrippa could use it to make hit-and-run raids on the other harbours. He could also attack and sink or drive away Cleopatra's supply ships from Egypt, with the result that Antony soon began to feel the effects

28 Coin of Antony and Cleopatra of 32 - 31, minted in Asia Minor.
  © *British Museum*

and had to resort to forced levies to form human convoys for food to be brought overland from Greece. Plutarch's great-grandfather was one of the unfortunate members of these teams, so in writing the life of Antony, Plutarch could relay the stories that had been passed down through his family.

With Agrippa now established in Greece and patrolling the seas, gaining more ground all the time, Octavian sailed with the bulk of his army across the Ionian sea, secured a landing, and took the opportunity while Antony's ships were called away from the naval base at Corcyra (Corfu) to seize the island. Octavian marched towards the Gulf of Ambracia and made a camp to the north of it, with protective walls extending to the sea to ensure that his supplies were delivered. In response Antony and Cleopatra came to Actium and set up camp on the southern arm of the two peninsulas that surrounded the Gulf. The two armies stared at each other and skirmished without much success. Agrippa gradually closed the sea lanes and bottled up the Antonian naval forces. He engaged part of Antony's fleet at Leucas and destroyed the ships, then he took Patrae where Antony and Cleopatra had spent the winter, and after that Corinth fell to him.

Antony's ships were now blockaded in the waters of the Gulf of Ambracia. He took a detachment of troops northwards to bring reinforcements from Macedonia and Thrace, and also to create a diversion, while Sosius tried to force a way through Agrippa's line of

29 Silver coin (denarius) issued by Antony in 31, portraying the goddess Victory and the head of the horned Jupiter Ammon, equating the Roman Jupiter with the eastern god Ammon. Antony's army was a mixed collection of Roman and eastern soldiers, so the appeal of these coins was as wide as he could make it. The legend round the head of the god describes Antony as consul for the third time in 31, and Imperator for the fourth time (M. ANTONIO. COS III. IMP. IIII). He had not been allowed to retain the consulship because Octavian deprived him of it, but Antony clung to his rightful office. The acclamation by the troops as Imperator was probably a result of the movement of the army onto the northern arm of the two peninsulas enclosing the Gulf of Ambracia, where Antony made camp for a while.
© British Museum

ships. When that attempt failed, Antony made sorties across the entrance to the Gulf to attack Octavian's camp. At least once he established a second camp of his own on the northern peninsula, but was eventually driven back to his first base. He tried to cut off Octavian's water supply, but failed. All his efforts are made to seem ineffective, bordering on the insane, but coin evidence shows that his legions hailed him as Imperator for the fourth time in 31. Soldiers of any period, ancient or modern, recognise successes and failures for what they are, and with the best will in the world, deflated troops cannot summon the energy to flatter a failed commander by spontaneously clamouring that he is a brilliant leader of men. The acclamation as Imperator was based on something solid, probably the expedition across the inlet and the establishment of a camp on the opposite side. At that point it probably seemed that Antony would beat off Octavian in a series of attacks, and the war would soon be at an end.

The fact that Antony remained on the northern peninsula for a while, and was encamped on its southern counterpart for some months indicates that what he achieved cannot have been quite as ineffective as the sources imply, but in the end he stayed too long. In the absence of a complete victory, he needed a short sharp blow, decisive enough to contain Octavian, and then he could either have broken out through the blockade or moved inland, forcing Octavian to attempt a land battle instead of a naval one. This is what Canidius urged him to do, when it was clear that they could not remain where they were indefinitely. Disease was a major threat, malaria was rife, supplies were low, and important men were beginning to desert. Even Domitius Ahenobarbus went over to Octavian; he was ill and died quite soon afterwards, but he had obviously reached the end of his patience and saw that Antony could not expect to win, only to escape. It was a heavy blow to Antony. He tried to restore discipline with harsh treatment of deserters or suspected discontents, but he only alienated people further. He put Iamblichus, king of the Arabians, to torture for disloyalty, and executed a Roman senator. The atmosphere in his camp turned very sour. Men would begin to ask themselves why they were doing all this, and what was it for ultimately, except to put the Queen of Egypt more securely on her throne, or to place either Antony or Octavian in a position of supreme power.

It was Cleopatra who argued, contrary to Canidius, that they should risk everything on a naval battle. Her reasons are not listed, but the fleet consisted largely of her ships, financed and manned by her money and her Egyptian sailors. In a way, both Canidius and Cleopatra were correct, in that something definite had to be done because the army and the fleet could not remain where they were. Cleopatra and Canidius argued for the methods that they knew best and trusted. Antony too will have analysed the situation of what he already knew. He may have reasoned that in the two previous civil wars, the invading force had won in land battles against the occupying force, and since he had been present for the campaign of Pharsalus and had won that of Philippi, he would be in a position to know who had the greater advantage. He knew that if he moved inland he may not have been able to persuade Octavian to give battle at all, so the army could march from place to place eating its way through Greece until it dropped from exhaustion. Moreover, if he was defeated in a land battle in Greece, the inevitable journey back to Egypt would be a long one, especially if the army was cut off from the coast, or the fleet was prevented from picking up the troops. Supplies would have to found on the march, and there could be no store system to support the army, unless the eastern cities were milked once more for money and food. Antony had devoted a great deal of time and effort to establishing good relations with many of these cities and minor states; if he forced them to supply his army in retreat, battered, wounded and hungry, everything would be undone in an instant. Nobody backs a loser if there is the slightest alternative, and the blindingly obvious alternative in this case would be to back the winner. Octavian's army would be close behind Antony's. City councils that wanted to make a good impression would close their gates to Antony, and wait until Octavian approached before they re-opened them. Worse still, if Cleopatra's and Antony's fleet had to be abandoned, there was the danger that Agrippa could sail direct to Alexandria, blockade it or even take it, making it very difficult to regain entry to Egypt

The long drawn-out struggle offered by a land battle probably repelled Antony. He had already spent months in deadlock, so the quick decision of a naval battle probably seemed the best one. He would either succeed in breaking through the blockade, extricate the fleet, and live to fight another day, or he would be defeated. Cleopatra will have had a great influence over him but Antony was still in command. If he had ordered a retreat into Greece, she had three choices, to follow him and take the risk of an arduous campaign, perhaps even being defeated with him, or she could act independently, using her fleet to escape to Egypt if she could break free; or she could attempt to strike a bargain with Octavian.

Antony knew that this would not be a decisive victory even if he won the battle or emerged from it relatively unscathed. He would have to find another base where he could regroup and fight again because Octavian would not let the matter drop. Egypt offered the safe haven that would give Antony and Cleopatra time to repair the damages, gather supplies and money, rest their army and fleet. But they all had to reach Egypt first, which would not be so easy. In choosing to fight at sea, the army had still to be catered for. It was not possible to transport all the troops on board ship, so Canidius was put in command of the whole army with orders to march overland to Egypt, while the sailors were ordered to carry their sails when they went into battle. This was unusual, and caused a stir. Antony said it was necessary to carry sails so that the fleet would be able to pursue the enemy as Agrippa fled before them. Probably no-one was fooled. On a practical level, the sailors would all know that a fresh offshore breeze often blew up in the afternoons which would give the ships extra speed to get away south-westwards, sparing the rowers. For that was all that could be hoped for, an escape. It began to look as though Antony was thinking only of himself and Cleopatra.

At this point Dellius, Antony's trusted envoy on several diplomatic missions, a close friend of his and an erstwhile admirer of Cleopatra, decided that he had better save himself now, rather than wait for what he considered an inevitable end. Dellius had a talent for self-preservation, pinpointing the right moment to change sides on two previous occasions. He sped to Octavian with Antony's battle plans and doubtless much useful information. He spread the word that he simply had to leave because Cleopatra was making plans to assassinate him. By this time his audience would swallow all this whole and beg for more. He would also be able to report that Antony did not have enough rowers to man all his ships, a fact that would be verified by the columns of smoke from burning vessels that Antony had to dispose of before he offered battle. Mixed emotions will have been engendered by this scene. Cleopatra had built up her fleet using imported timber and Egyptian wealth, and now it was ashes. Antony had tried to defend the coast with a magnificent collection of ships, only to witness Agrippa rapidly rounding them all up like sheep, disposing of some and penning the rest. And Octavian had risked a great deal to bring his rivals to this desperate situation, and had succeeded.

On 2 September 31 Antony and Cleopatra emerged from the waters of the Gulf of Ambracia, the remains of their fleet sailing through the narrow opening and fanning out to meet Octavian's in the open sea beyond. Agrippa and Octavian spread out in front of Antony and waited. Cleopatra's ships were in the rear, behind Antony's centre. On board her flagship she carried all the money and treasure, so it was not part of the plan for her squadron to be in the thick of the fighting. As the day progressed, the two fleets sat and stared at each other for some time, then Antony moved forwards. He could not go back into the shelter of the Gulf, but Octavian and Agrippa did not engage in battle, so Antony had to force the issue. It meant that he had to move further out than he intended and risk being outflanked. He commanded the right, opposite Agrippa, and the two lines stretched further and further

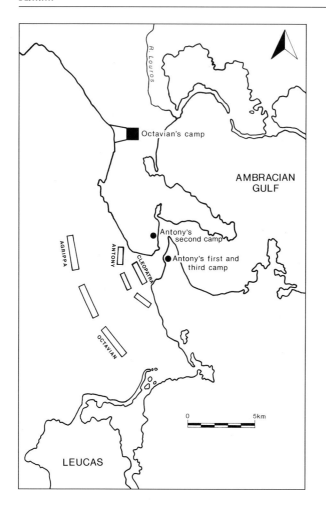

30 *The battle of Actium, fought on 2 September 31. Antony ordered his ship's captains to carry their sails with them, which was an unusual command when the fleet was to go into action, but since he could not hope to win the battle, he needed to extricate as many of his ships as he could and sail away. He came out with three squadrons facing those of Octavian and Agrippa, and tried to turn Agrippa's squadron by extending his own line northwards. The plan did not work, but Octavian's centre was stretched out and weakened, and Cleopatra seized her chance to escape by suddenly pressing on through Antony's ships, then Octavian's, and on into the open sea. She carried the war chest on board her flagship, so her escape was vital. The other ships fared less well, and could not escape. Some went back into the harbour, overwhelmed by the numerical superiority of Octavian's galleys, and only a small percentage of Antony's and Cleopatra's fleet survived to reach Egypt. Drawn by Graeme Stobbs*

out to avoid being turned. The centre squadrons of each fleet were locked in battle and their lines thinned out slightly. Cleopatra seized her chance, pressed on through Antony's ships, then though Octavian's into the open sea. She was heading for Egypt. As Michael Grant points out, this was part of the plan, to give her the chance to sail away to safety with the treasure chest in order to lay the foundations for the renewal of the war, and the reception of Antony's battered fleet, if the ships could disengage and get away.

It was said that Cleopatra had deserted Antony in his hour of need, that perhaps she thought that he was dead, and so on; there were many other variations on this theme. Antony laid himself open to charges that he favoured Cleopatra and sacrificed his soldiers and sailors to ensure her safety. It seemed that he too had abandoned his fleet when he transferred to a smaller and faster craft and followed Cleopatra. In the end that was all he could do. He had probably planned to break out himself to create a gap for his other ships to disengage and sail into open water, but Octavian's fleet was larger, and Antony's ships could not pass through. Many were sunk, and some turned back to harbour, where the chances of escaping were reduced to nil. They surrendered to Octavian because there was no point in doing anything else. Antony escaped with perhaps fifty ships.

According to Plutarch, Antony spent days on the deck of Cleopatra's flag ship, not speaking to anyone. Retrospective knowledge gives the impression that all was lost at Actium, and tradition has embellished the battle until it has achieved the status of a decisive turning point in the history not only of Octavian's rise to sole power, but of the western world in general. But in the days that followed 2 September 31, it would not be viewed in such a crystal clear light. Antony had broken the blockade and rescued some ships, and his war chest; he was heading for a secure base where more money and supplies were assured; and his army was marching through Macedonia into Asia Minor and thence to Egypt.

More battles would assuredly have to be fought, but there was a breathing space for both armies. Octavian managed to lure Antony's army away from Canidius by bribery, so that gave him an enormous advantage, but not yet an overwhelming one. He wintered on the island of Samos, but there was trouble in Italy to which he had to attend first before he could continue the war. He was not yet in total control in Rome, where Antony still had some sympathisers, and even if they were indifferent to Antony, not all men were as solidly behind Octavian as his later assertions would have his contemporaries and posterity believe. The son of Lepidus tried to raise a revolt against Octavian, and caused enough problems to force Agrippa and then Octavian himself to return to the city.

In the meantime, Antony and Cleopatra sailed towards Egypt but did not go immediately to Alexandria. They needed time to compose themselves, especially since by the time they reached the coast of North Africa, they will doubtless have heard of the desertion of the army to Octavian. They landed at a small harbour at Paraetonium, to the west of Alexandria, then split up. Antony stayed there for a while, leaving Cleopatra to enter Alexandria alone. Perhaps it was prearranged, or perhaps by now Antony was as depressed as Plutarch says he was. Entering Alexandria without him, Cleopatra put out all the banners and turned her arrival into a victory parade. Normal human beings would show some traces of the strains of a sea voyage preceded by a wearisome campaign of deadlocked struggling, but Cleopatra knew what her role dictated and played it to perfection. The first appearance in Alexandria was magnificent, not perhaps too much of a taxing performance in itself, but once having arrived, she then had to keep it up permanently, and set in motion more preparations for war. And now she was alone, fighting not just for Egypt, or for herself, but trying to support Antony as well, whose resolve had melted away. When he did come to Alexandria, he withdrew to a building on a little spur of land on the shore line, and called it the Timoneum. Antony had received a classical education. He was referring to Timon of Athens, a famous hermit, who had turned his back on the rest of human kind.

It was left to Cleopatra to organise for war, and for political strength in Egypt. She brought her son Caesarion and Antony's eldest son Antyllus into the public eye. Caesarion was now invested as Ptolemy XV, and Antyllus, aged about fourteen, celebrated his coming of age as an adult, by exchanging his child's clothing for the dress of a man, the *toga virilis*. These public ceremonies were declarations of future solidity, not yet a handing down of power, but an unequivocal affirmation that there were to be successors, and a message to potential usurpers that all was still as it had been and would ever be. There were not only the inhabitants of Egypt to think of, but also the alliances with eastern states that could not be allowed to waver. If there was the slightest hint that Cleopatra was weakened the network would begin to unravel as

31 *Bronze rostrum, or ship's beak attached to the prow to strengthen it, making an*
   effective ramming device with which to sink enemy vessels. This rostrum was found
   in the bay at Actium, and is now in the British Museum, London.
   © *British Museum*

opportunists dashed for the main chance, either to attain independence
and take over revenues, or to take independence one stage further and
to make war. One of the first measures that Cleopatra took on her
arrival in Alexandria was to execute Artavasdes of Armenia, who had
been taken prisoner by Antony but allowed to live in gilded captivity in
Egypt. This was a definite political move to demonstrate her solidarity
with Media, the natural enemy of Armenia. The alliance arranged by
Antony between Cleopatra and the Median king had been sealed by the
betrothal of his daughter to Alexander Helios. Mindful of the future of
her children if not of herself, Cleopatra preserved as much goodwill as
she could. There was precious little of it left to her. As Octavian
approached Egypt, and it was only a matter of time before he did, many
an eastern ruler would find it more convenient to look to him for an

alliance rather than Antony and Cleopatra. Not only the kings and princes were disaffected, but also most Romans in the eastern provinces from the lowliest officials to the governors themselves would all be forced to examine their political situations, and make a decision as to whether Octavian or Antony would offer the best chance of survival or promotion. All over the east, there was a great restlessness and uncertainty, which Octavian could exploit to his own advantage, promising rewards that were not yet in his gift, either politically or financially, but if he emerged successful from the war, he had every chance of profiting from the wealth of Egypt, and from the political status that would accrue as the defender of Rome. It was a gamble well worth the risk, and if he did not emerge successfully, then it would not matter what he had promised. Cleopatra was of the same matrix as Octavian, shrewd, opportunistic and willing to gamble, so she would understand perfectly how he would operate. At a time when she knew that she herself and Antony were under threat, Cleopatra had to maintain an impenetrable facade of supreme confidence and authority.

She perhaps derived great comfort from the news that the people of Upper Egypt were prepared to rise up in arms to fight on her behalf. At least her efforts to integrate them into her realm and to speak their language would have reaped its rewards, had she chosen to accept. But she declined to involve civilians in war. It would have been an uneven fight, perhaps long and drawn out, but it would bring great destruction even if she won the battles, and if she lost, then Octavian would be at liberty to wreak revenge on the ordinary people. If they remained quiet, their way of life could continue, except that they would pay their taxes to a new Roman ruler. Realistically, Cleopatra knew that she could not win this war. If she managed to beat off Octavian, there would be no lasting peace because there would always be new enemies in Rome ready to take up the challenge.

The anticipation of ultimate defeat pervaded the whole of Antony's circle. In place of the 'Inimitable Livers' he had formed a society of 'Inseparables at Death'. He had given money to all those who wished to leave because he did not want to force them to fight a battle that he thought was already lost. Desertions became more frequent as Octavian closed in. After he had quelled the disturbances in Rome at the end of 31, Octavian returned to the unfinished war in the spring of 30. By early summer he was on the coast of Phoenicia. He had been collecting new allies ever since he wintered at Samos, so his progress through the eastern territories was not only unhindered, but positively encouraged. Herod of Judaea, who was grateful to Antony but had no reason to be faithful to Cleopatra, had offered an alliance with Octavian soon after Actium, and now assisted his army on the march. Embassies from Cleopatra and Antony appeared at Octavian's camp, but he gave no definite answers to their offers of peace and their requests that they should be allowed to retire into private life. Cleopatra sent gifts, and offered to abdicate if her children could be installed as rulers in her place. Antony's son Antyllus arrived with quantities of money to plead his father's cause. These actions brought Antony and Cleopatra no credit, even if their main motives were to spare their friends and their troops from the horrors of war. It must be questioned whether the stories are entirely trustworthy. It is unlikely that they are complete inventions, though the ancient sources may have exaggerated the details. The options open to Antony and Cleopatra were very few, but by their offers to retire into private life, they advertised to Octavian how desperate was their situation. It revealed that they could not make a stand because they could not rely upon their armies, and had nowhere to go except to stay in Egypt. It is said that Cleopatra made preparations to escape to the far east via the Red Sea, and that she had ships waiting there which were destroyed by Malchus, the king of Nabataea. She sent Caesarion eastwards for his safety and perhaps intended to join him, but in the end she did not leave Alexandria.

While Octavian approached Egypt over land from the east, his lieutenant Cornelius Gallus approached by sea from the west. It seemed that they were invincible. When Octavian reached Pelusium the commander of the garrison, Seleucus, failed to stop him. He may have fought and been defeated or he may have simply opened the gates. Cleopatra executed his wife and daughter. Antony took forty ships to block Gallus but was defeated; he lost the ships and the landing place at Paraetonium. This left only the Delta and Alexandria itself, boxed in on both sides by Octavian's troops. The tragedy was drawing to its inevitable close, though Octavian's icy calm was slightly disturbed by the possibility that Cleopatra might destroy her treasure before he could lay hands on it. According to Plutarch he now began to communicate with her, offering lenient terms. Antony responded by offering to commit suicide if this would persuade Octavian to spare Cleopatra. At one point, probably now, it is said that Octavian promised to spare her if she would surrender Antony, but she refused. The

32 Silver coin of about 30, displaying a fine portrait of Cleopatra as Queen, at a time when she needed to assert her authority very strongly. Cabinet des Médailles, Paris. Photo Jean Roubier

nobility of these actions validates the enduring love story, Antony prepared to give up his life for her sake, and Cleopatra determined not to save herself by sacrificing him. It is also an enduring tragedy, made even greater by the fact that, absorbed in themselves, they had not yet realised that Octavian was not interested in either of them. They had faded into insignificance, because he had already won the war against them when he converted them into enemies of Rome. Octavian had already dismissed them, and their children, because he wanted Egypt.

For a brief moment, Antony reverted to his old self. When Octavian's cavalry approached the city from the east, he dashed out of the Canopus gate and routed them. He returned to Cleopatra and celebrated a victory, but by now they must have known that all was lost. Neither the army nor the fleet had any fighting spirit left, desertions were rife, and the promises of wealth that Antony had made to subvert Octavian's legions had not produced any results. On the last day of July, Antony feasted well, prepared for battle next day. He knew that he had no hope of victory, so he probably was not in the least surprised when reports reached him that a ghostly procession had been heard but not seen leaving the city by the eastern gate, to the strains of beautiful, haunting music. The gods always deserted a city as it was about to fall, so he knew now that Dionysus and his revellers had departed.

Next day, the fleet and the army engaged Octavian's troops. The two fleets never exchanged blows, but sailed towards each other and merged. Presumably there had been many an exchange between ships' captains during the previous days, as to who was the most likely winner. Antony's ships had been badly mauled by Octavian's at Actium. To fight now for no appreciable results would have been a waste of time. When the legions saw what was happening at sea, they too ceased hostilities. Some soldiers ran away, while others simply laid down their weapons. Antony rode back to the Royal Palace, allegedly accusing Cleopatra of betraying him. Why he should think so is probably attributable to despair; it was too late now even for betrayal.

While the desultory battles were fought, Cleopatra left the Palace and barricaded herself and her maids inside her mausoleum. It is not certain if she intended to kill herself immediately, or to wait for news of Antony, but whatever her intentions, Antony though that she was already dead. Everything was lost, the city lay wide open for Octavian to take it, so his only choices involved death or dishonour. He chose the former. His servant Eros refused to help him to commit suicide and killed himself instead. Antony fell on his sword, but did not die immediately, so he was still conscious when Cleopatra's secretary Diomedes found him, to tell him that Cleopatra was waiting for him.

The doors to the mausoleum were closed, so Antony was hauled up to the upper floor on a stretcher and dragged in through the window. He probably did not live long, and probably did die in Cleopatra's arms. What their state of mind must have been can only be imagined; no wonder that the scenario has proved so attractive to writers, playwrights, artists, and film producers. Cleopatra had little bargaining power left, and was at the mercy of Octavian, who kept sending messengers to her to reason with her, but for what purpose is not known. The story goes that Octavian was anxious to take her alive to walk behind his triumphal chariot in Rome, and that she thwarted him by secretly arranging her suicide, but it is open to question whether Octavian planned such an end for her. By dragging her through Rome he would vindicate himself for the war-mongering against Rome's so-called worst enemy, but then he would have to execute her or keep her a prisoner in Rome or in Italy, converting her from enemy to martyr in the process. If she were allowed to live, there was the possibility of uprisings to put her back on the throne. If she survived, wherever she was imprisoned, the fate of Egypt would be less clear cut than if she and her children were eradicated, and it was Egypt that Octavian wanted, far more than any splendid triumph in Rome.

Remaining in her tomb for the next few days, Cleopatra was watched by Octavian's men. She was allowed out to attend to Antony's funeral, and then brought under guard to the Royal Palace. She probably thought of the different circumstances in which she had lived there with Caesar, two decades before. She may have held an audience with Octavian, to bargain for fair treatment of the people of Egypt, for whom she had always held respect. There were rebellions in Upper Egypt in her name, so it is possible that she was anxious to spare her supporters unnecessary suffering when there was nothing to be gained from it. There is no tradition of such bargaining in the ancient sources, but it would be the final measure she could attempt when she knew that Octavian was going to take over her kingdom.

Her resolve to kill herself was no doubt already formed. It remained to find a method. The legend says that she died by the bite of the poisonous asp, hidden in a basket of figs. She probably chose this method herself, since the bite of the asp was said to confer immortality on the victim, and more importantly the snake was one of the emblems of Isis, with whom Cleopatra identified herself throughout her reign. Her deification and immortal status ought to have been automatic in normal times, but these were not normal times, so she probably wanted to ensure that all went as it should when she died.

She prepared for death dressed in truly regal fashion, conscious to the bitter end of her Royal image. She owed it to Egypt to die as she had lived, in splendour and wealth; to die defeated was honourable enough, but to die in rags, broken in spirit would have negated her whole existence. It was her last gesture, as strong a defiance of her fate as she could muster. Just before she died she sent a messenger with a sealed letter to Octavian, asking him to honour her wishes and bury her at Antony's side, which to his credit, he did. No-one knows where the two are buried, but there have been so many exciting new discoveries in the sunken ancient harbour of Alexandria, that it is always possible that the tomb may come to light.

It was probably a great relief to Octavian that Cleopatra chose to end her life magnificently and so conveniently soon after the fall of Alexandria. Her continued survival would have been an embarrassment. He pretended to be surprised that she had killed herself, and said that he had sent for the psylli, the snake-charmers, to suck out the poison, but since it was supposed to be a shock to him that she was dead, it is odd that he knew exactly how Cleopatra had chosen to die. Her death released him from all obligation. He took over the kingdom as his own preserve, installing Cornelius Gallus as its governor. Gallus was only a middle-class officer, an eques, not a senator, so this was an unprecedented arrangement, but if it was adopted for sheer convenience on the spur of the moment, perhaps to reward Gallus for his efforts in leading ships and troops into Alexandria from the east, then it suited Octavian's purpose both then and for ever afterwards. The equestrian career structure evolved under successive Emperors after Octavian-Augustus established its foundations, and the post of Prefect of Egypt was the pinnacle, achieved by only the most fortunate equestrians. The Prefect was answerable to the Emperor and not to the Senate, and no senator was even allowed to visit Egypt without express Imperial permission. This highlights the importance of Egypt to Octavian and his successors, who guarded themselves well against the possibility that any noble Romans might raise revolt there and utilise the wealth of the county to finance an army and to buy the loyalty of Roman generals and eastern kings.

When Antony and Cleopatra were both dead, Octavian had only a few matters to attend to in order to assume total supremacy. He ordered a search for Caesarion and had him killed. An exact chronology is not established, so it cannot be ascertained whether Cleopatra knew of the death of her son before she died herself, or whether she went to her death confident that she had successfully arranged for his escape and survival. The fate of her other children is not fully documented. Cleopatra Selene may have been taken to Rome and raised by Octavia, with Antony's other children. Eventually she was married to king Juba of Mauretania, and went to live in North

33 Octavian, the victor of the battle of Actium soon carried the war to Alexandria, which fell on 1 August 30. Octavian issued commemorative coins three years later in 27 when his supremacy was an acknowledged fact. He chose the crocodile as an appropriate and neutral Egyptian symbol, for by this time he could afford to be magnanimous to Cleopatra and her memory, so he had no need to advertise the fact that his victory was really over her as Queen of Egypt. He proclaimed that he had captured Egypt (AEGYPT CAPTA) and styled himself simply but effectively as 'son of the divine Caesar, consul for the seventh time' (CAESAR. DIVI.F.COS. VII). © British Museum

Africa. Alexander Helios and Ptolemy Philadelphus may have gone with her, but they are not heard of again, after the fall of Alexandria. Antony's teenage son Antyllus, declared his heir and portrayed on Antony's coins, was killed in Alexandria on Octavian's orders, perhaps as soon as the city fell on 2 August 30. All Antony's other children survived, brought up in close proximity to Octavian and his court circle. His two daughters, both named Antonia, were the ancestors of Emperors of Rome, the younger daughter being the mother of Claudius and the grandmother of Caligula, and the elder the grandmother of Nero. These latter two descendants were hardly a credit to their great-grandfather Antony, but Claudius was a learned scholar and a capable administrator, who enlarged the harbour at Ostia and added Britain to the Empire, completing projects that Caesar had started, altogether a worthy successor to Antony.

Cleopatra's memory was not erased. The statue placed by Caesar in the temple of Venus Genetrix remained there, and it is said that a certain Archibius, an official of Cleopatra's court paid Octavian 1000 talents in return for saving her portraits and statues. In victory Octavian could afford to be generous, maintaining an ambivalent attitude towards Cleopatra. She was Rome's enemy, to be feared and abhorred, but there was a nobility about her and a strength of mind and determination that Romans could not fail to admire. There were seven Cleopatras in all, but despite their achievements, the six preceding ones pale into nonentities compared to the last. When anyone in the western world utters the name of Cleopatra, the majority of listeners think of only one, exotic, attractive, magnificent, and a woman.

Bibliography

A Note on the Ancient Sources

There is no single ancient source for the life of Cleopatra, which is somewhat surprising in view of the fact that she is so well-known in modern times. She is mentioned in the works of several ancient authors, but even then her life is not documented from beginning to end in any coherent fashion, and most of the stories about her are of the fabulous or anecdotal kind.

Contemporaries who knew her and wrote about her include Julius Caesar, the tutor of her children Nicolaus of Damascus, and Herod, king of Judaea. The historian Asinius Pollio lived through the civil wars between Pompey and Caesar and Octavian and Antony, and wrote an account of his times that extended probably to the mid thirties BC. Of these, Caesar's narrative of the Alexandrian war gives scarcely any detail of Cleopatra as a person, and mentions her only in passing, and the work of Nicolaus and the memoirs of Herod are known only in quotation in other authors' works. Asinius Pollio's work is also lost, save for a few fragments contained in other writings. Marcus Tullius Cicero knew Cleopatra from her time in Rome as Caesar's guest, and though he wrote of her in his letters to Atticus, there is little in the way of solid information about her, only gossip, unexplained allusions and occasionally prejudice.

Later authors who mentioned Cleopatra were already imbued with the Augustan tradition that she was the greatest enemy that Rome ever faced. They were also hostile to Antony. Titus Livius (Livy) and Velleius Paterculus both pleaded the cause of Octavian-Augustus, and in turn downgraded the achievements of Antony and Cleopatra. Livy's history covered the period but this part of his work has not survived. Velleius' work is an abbreviated account that denies any credit at all to

Antony and Cleopatra. The Jewish historian Flavius Josephus, who wrote in the first century AD, is hostile to Cleopatra on behalf of king Herod, whose territories she is said to have desired, and has no good word to say of her.

Much of the information about the life of Cleopatra derives from Plutarch's *Life of Antony* where he waxes lyrical about the more fabulous of Cleopatra's attributes and activities. Plutarch was born about 70 to 80 years after the deaths of Cleopatra and Antony, and had access to some first-hand information passed down from relatives and friends who had witnessed events or even known or seen the Queen herself. The narrative is an entertaining read, and inspired Shakespeare, so it is from these two sources that the western tradition about Cleopatra derives.

Much of the Augustan literature on the period presents Cleopatra in an ambivalent light, condemning her alleged hostility to Rome and her acquisitive territorial ambitions, but admiring her determination and bravery. Quintus Horatius Flaccus (Horace) and Vergilius Maro (Vergil) refer to the Queen in sometimes indirect allusions, but spread a general picture of danger from the most artful woman of her age. Current opinion denies that these poets were closely directed by Augustus himself, scarcely able to write a word unless he vetted it first, but nonetheless, in general they take the line that Augustus saved the world from a dire threat.

Background information on the period can be found in the works of Appian, who wrote in the second century AD, and Cassius Dio, whose work belongs to the third century. Their own sources will have included the lost works referred to above, but they do not always acknowledge the source from which they drew their material.

Besides the works of the ancient authors, there are the official administrative sources, not abundant for the reign of Cleopatra, comprising papyri, inscriptions, sculptures and coins. As archaeological excavations progress in Alexandria and elsewhere, it is likely that more of this sort of material will come to light, to be added to the corpus of knowledge already gleaned from these useful tools. Portraits of Cleopatra are not numerous, and not always securely identified, but from her unflattering coin-portraits comparison can be made with her distinctive Alexandrian hairstyle and her prominent nose.

Cleopatra as she emerges from the available information is comparable to the internationally famous film-stars of the great age of cinema, so extremely well-known, yet so elusive, fascinating to ancient and modern authors alike. There are a great number of books and articles about Cleopatra, but not all of them restrict themselves to a description of her life and times. She has been depicted through the ages by the important artists of the western world, and a great number of books are concerned only with the Shakespearian Cleopatra, and not with the Queen of Egypt who existed alongside Caesar, Antony and Octavian. This bibliography groups titles under broad general headings, in order to distinguish the strictly biographical material from the art history and literary assessments.

Ancient sources

These works are available in the Loeb Classical Library, which provides a Greek or Latin text with a parallel English translation and relevant footnotes.

Appian	*Roman History* (Loeb vols. 2-4)
Caesar	*Alexandrian War*
Cicero	*Letters to Atticus* (3 vols)
Dio	*Roman History* (Loeb vols 3-6)
Horace	*Carmen Saeculare*
	Odes
Josephus	*Jewish Antiquities*
	Jewish War
Plutarch	*Life of Antony*
Velleius Paterculus	*Roman History*
Vergil	*Aeneid*
	Georgics

Modern Works

Biographies

Bradford, E	*Cleopatra*. Hodder and Stoughton 1971
Fielding, S	*The Lives of Cleopatra and Octavia*. London 1928
Foss, M	*The Search for Cleopatra*. Michael O'Mara Books 1997
Grant, M	*Cleopatra*. Weidenfeld and Nicolson 1972 (Excellent, especially on source material)
Lindsay, J	*Cleopatra*. Constable 1971

Mundy, T	*Queen Cleopatra*. London 1929
Payen, L	*Cleopatra*. New York 1915
Weigall, A	*The Life and Times of Cleopatra*. London 1914

Historical Background

Cambridge Ancient History Vol. IX The Roman Republic 133–44 BC ed. S A Cook et al. Cambridge University Press 1932

Cambridge Ancient History Vol. X The Augustan Empire 43 BC–AD69 ed. A K Bowman et al. Cambridge University Press second edition 1997 (The first edition 1934 is still useful)

Bell, H Idris	*Egypt From Alexander the Great to the Arab Conquest*. Oxford University Press 1938
Carter, J M	*The Battle of Actium*. Hamish Hamilton 1970
Earl, D	*The Age of Augustus*. Elek 1968, reprinted by Ferndale editions 1980
Empereur, J-Y	*Alexandria Rediscovered*. British Museum Press 1998
Grant, M	*Roman History from Coins*. Cambridge University Press 1968
Gruen, E S	*The Last Generation of the Roman Republic*. University of California Press 1974; reprinted in paperback 1995
Gurval, R A	*Actium and Augustus: the politics and emotions of civil war*. University of Michigan Press 1995
La Riche, W	*Alexandria: the sunken city*. Weidenfeld and Nicolson 1996
Meier, C	*Caesar*. Harper Collins 1995
Scullard, H H	*From the Gracchi to Nero*. Methuen 3rd ed 1970
Southern, P	*Augustus*. Routledge 1998
Southern, P	*Mark Antony*. Tempus 1998
Stockton, D	*Cicero: a political biography*. Oxford University Press 1970
Syme, R	*The Roman Revolution*. Oxford University Press 1939
Weigall, A	*Mark Antony: his life and times*. London 1931

Cleopatra in Art and Literature

Cook, J	*Women in Shakespeare*. London 1980
Curl, J S	*The Egyptian Revival*. London 1982
Flamarion, E	*Cleopatra: from history to legend*. Thames and Hudson 1997
Hamer, M	*Signs of Cleopatra*. Routledge 1992
Hughes-Hallett, L	*Cleopatra: histories, dreams and distortions*. Pimlico 1990

Index